To Nell
Dec 25th 1875

IRISH ODES

AND

OTHER POEMS.

BY

AUBREY DE VERE.

NEW-YORK:
THE CATHOLIC PUBLICATION SOCIETY,
126 NASSAU STREET.

1869.

JOHN A. GRAY & GREEN,
Printers and Stereotypers,
16 and 18 Jacob Street, New-York.

TO

HENRY WADSWORTH LONGFELLOW,

THIS VOLUME IS DEDICATED

BY

AUBREY DE VERE.

PREFACE.

WISH has sometimes been expressed by my American friends that an edition of my poems should be published in their country. No one who has written in the English language, whether with the lower or the higher aims of literature, can fail to desire that his works should have a circulation in America. That country must ere long contain far the larger number of those who speak English; in it, despite those material interests which imperiously demand the attention of a young country, poetry has already been produced with an abundance, and read with an eagerness, rare in the old world; and it cannot be doubted that every liberal art must achieve new triumphs amid a race dowered with all that can develop moral and social energies, and naught that can depress intellect or divide brethren. The Liberal Arts are the children of a virtuous, unboastful Liberty, frank-hearted, and not self-respecting alone, but full of respect for all that is human. Their larger growths are quickened from the soil of sympathies wide as the earth, and are freshened by aspirations not restrained to the earth. Like the spontaneous growths of Nature, they are also in part, it is true, Traditions; but the allegation that America must wait long for a past, is an error. She has only to *remember*, as well as look forward, and the Past of all those nations from which her race is derived is her Past also.

For me the question is not merely one of Literature. There now exist in America more of my Irish fellow-countrymen than remain in their native country; and I cannot but wish that my Poetry, much of which illustrates their History and Religion, should reach those Irish "of the dispersion" in that land which has extended to them its hospitality. Whoever loves that people must follow it in its wanderings with an earnest desire that, upon whatever shore the storms may have cast it, and by whatever institutions it may be cherished or proved, it may retain with vigilant fidelity, and be valued for retaining, those among its characteristics which most belong to the Ireland of History and Religion. The Irish character is one easily mistaken by the "rough and ready" philosophy of the caricaturist. "A little part, and that the worst, he sees." To the rest he has not the key. Broad farce, and broad romance, have familiarized men with its coarser traits. Its finer reveal themselves to poetry. She deals with what lies beneath the surface. She makes her study, not of the tavern, but of the hill-side chapel, and of the cottage-hearth without stain and faithful to the departed. She ponders the tear-blotted letter, and the lip-worn rosary. In a face seldom joyless, but not seldom overcast, she finds something which makes her tread the wanderer's native land, and share with him the recollections of the Past. Those recollections, dear to all deep-hearted Races, but dearest to the saddest, have to the Irish been a reality in times when the present seemed a dream. But hitherto they have also been vindictive. Now that a Sectarian Ascendency is on the point of ceasing, they will lose their bitterness wherever the old and true Irish character remains. That character is generous where love is not curdled into hate by wrong. To attain Civil Freedom and Religious Equality was long the task which nature and duty imposed upon Ireland. To develop, and rightly to direct the energies, moral, intellectual, and industrial, of a People set free, must ere long become the task of a thoughtful patriotism. These convictions will be traced in the poems which give the present volume its name, and occupy its earlier portion—poems written at various periods, but, like those in the latter part of the volume, not included in the writer's previous publications. The intermediate poems are a selection from his works.

It is sometimes said that the poetry of a Catholic, even when its subjects are, as in the present instance, mainly secular, should not expect an impartial audience in a country predominantly Protestant. The remark can hardly be one of universal application. Religious jealousies, now in most countries happily on the wane, are not produced by diversities of Faith; they are but social passions or panics—an after-swell bequeathed by the political tempests of past times. America, since she became a nation, has never persecuted, and therefore can afford to be just. Let it be for her to teach the world that true liberty—the liberty which accords all that it demands—has no better friend than true Catholicity. The age is one of progress; Catholicity has much that is in direct harmony with its furthest and hardiest aspirations, and as much that is indirectly supplemental to them. It fears no progress that is not downward. It loves the people; it sojourned with them in the Catacombs; it delivered them from Pagan Imperialism, protected them from the Mahometan yoke, and struck from them the chains of Feudal serfdom. It rejoices in the expansion of their justly-regulated rights and powers, in which, as in a dilated breast, its free spirit respires with ease. But it also hallows Authority. It asserts Equality, not in the form of a surly and barren independence, but in that of a reciprocal dependence fruitful in mutual good. It emancipates us first from lawless passions, and next from those lawless tyrannies which are at once their offspring and their punishment; but it works these marvellous works only because it pays and demands an allegiance based neither on a servile nor a selfish motive, and therefore unaggrieved and unashamed. It generates a reverential good-will which, as by an inner law, subdues the aggressions of selfishness, and gives to each man a protector in his neighbor ; but it at the same time takes from external laws its sting by creating the virtue of a proud and generous loyalty. That loyalty looks on the State not as a mere aggregate, the administrator of Society's material interests, but as the sacred unity of a nation, the majestic inheritor of its duties, the vindicator of a Divine Justice—nay, as, in its vastness and its permanence, a shadow of the Universal Church. Yet it remembers that to a loyal People the loyalty of the State is also due. We are made up of habits. Man requires both obedience and liberty: and it is where the priceless freedom of the heart is sustained by a willing and reasonable obedience in the spiritual sphere, that liberty, civil and social, can walk securely while steadied by the lightest yoke. In the Church History of 1800 years there needs little ingenuity to find some matter for reproach, and much for cavil. That period, however, during which the most devoted asserters of liberty have learned to confess that the Church was its surest friend, exceeds threefold the time during which they maintain that she acted but as a drag upon the wheels of progress. The road of Progress is a long road, and if on parts of it there had been no drag, perhaps no wheels would have remained for that portion which lies open before the Intelligence of the Future.

We are sometimes told that, in our day, Poetry which does not affect the "sensational" must not hope to be popular. The "sensational" includes several schools, the worst of which is that one which is sensual as well as sensational. The fanatics of this school declaim about Passion; but they mean by the word little more than Appetite intellectualized. Far other was the meaning of Milton, when he described Poetry as a thing "simple, sensuous, and *impassioned;*" for it was he who characterized specially the stately and severe Greek Tragedy, as "high actions, and high *passions* best describing." Neither did he use the word "sensuous" in opposition to that lofty doctrine of Bacon, who affirms that Poetry "subjects the shews of things to the *desires* of the *mind.*" Milton but intended thus to contrast Poetry with Science, which last has been well said to draw up the exterior universe into that of Thought and Law, whereas it is the office of Poetry to embody the interior world of Thought in palpable form. The great master of Inductive Philosophy was, in this matter, Idealist; while the great Idealist confessed, perhaps against the tenor of his habitual sympathies, the objective character of Poetry; but these two authentic canons of criticism set forth but the same philosophy as regarded from two opposite points of view, the one insisting that the soul of Poetry is Thought, the other adding that for that soul a body exists also.

Let not the Sensationalists of this school imagine that Passion is their characteristic. It belongs to their narrow domain neither exclusively nor inclusively. True Passion finds its sustenance everywhere—in every joy and woe of humanity—in the faith and patience of oppressed nations, and the cry from the lonely hearth—in the

> "sanguine flower inscribed with woe,"*

and in the yew-grove,

> "as if for festal purpose decked
> with *unrejoicing* berries."†

False Passion, in its ultimate development, loathes all food but carrion, and destroys all that a sane heart reveres. It ignores the affections

* Milton. † Wordsworth.

and values the passions themselves but for the mud turned up by the storm. Its wit is maliciousness, and its humor but the pretext for license. It blots even from material nature her beauty ; for it abolishes, in its gross delineations, all her variety and harmony of expression, as well as all that gradation which metes and measures human enjoyment. Resolving all things into the senses, it stultifies the senses themselves, which for man have no true existence except in so far as they receive and give forth subordinately to man's higher Powers. It overruns whatever is fresh, and tramples down whatever is sweet. It rushes over God's world like a conflagration, licking up those innumerable half lights and half shades, precious alike in their reserve and their disclosures, through which the beauty of nature is rendered infinite, and her bounty inexhaustible. It leaves behind it nothing but blackness and barrenness. It may content itself with the suggestive, and conceal beneath the whitened outside of decorous language the implication that dares not be named ; or it may boast that it is natural, because it has renounced faith in the primary instincts of the moral nature, that it may celebrate animal instincts in language that knows itself to be naked, and is not ashamed; or it may endeavor to galvanize dead Art with the spasmodic tricks of spurious Science, exhibiting the malformations of depraved fancy, or of nature disnatured, in psychological poems and philosophic "Etudes," revolting as those anatomical eccentricities ranged round the walls of a museum:—to such achievements it may rise; but it has forfeited all heritage in the two great homes of authentic poetry—man's heart and the universe of God. The sensual-sensational cannot plead the excuse of a tender weakness. It is essentially the heartless. In it the pathetic has no part. To feel anything it must have nails driven into it. In it love has no part; for it has broken loose from that Reverence which is itself but Love shrouded beneath her sacred and protecting veil, and from that moral sense from which, and not from the animal nature or a blind caprice, the genuine human affections are outgrowths. In it the imagination has no part—that large and free imagination which aspires to breathe the spiritual into the material, not to merge the former in the latter. In her forest-pleasaunce there remains not a tree that is not branded nor a spring that is not brackish.

Literary heresies, like religions, attract at first through their supposed originality. "Sensationalism" in this form—for I do not speak of those which offend only against refinement—fancies that it has discovered a new sort of "muscular" literature. It is new in nothing but the circumstances which aggravate the offence. The better time of Paganism itself was a reproach to the worst times of countries nominally Christian; and it was only when the higher genius of the ancient world had been blighted by bad morals and despotic Governments, that sensuality usurped upon its literature. Cast down from its Pagan throne, and remanded to the reptile form, it worked up again even in the ages of Faith, creeping back into the precinct made pure, and blending, in a half merry, half mystical libertinage, the higher thoughts of a chivalrous time with the renewed revolt of fallen nature. To what extent the corrupt element in the Fabliaux, Tales, and Troubadour songs of the Middle Ages defrauded the world of that complete Mediæval literature of which the "Vita Nuova" was the snowy bud, and the "Divina Commedia" the half-opened flower, we shall probably never know; but what Dante did the writers of the "Novelle" undid, and in Chaucer's poetry a dark stream ran side by side with the clear one. For a long time a childlike Faith made head against a childish instability and inconsistency as to right and wrong; but by degrees the loftier element evaporated, while the coarser residuum remained behind. In ages of less simplicity the same evil has again and again recurred, marring the heroic strength of Elizabethan drama, scattering plague-spots over the dreary revel of Charles the Second, and in France pushing aside the Bossuets and Racines, and sealing a large part of literature, by its own confession, against the young and the innocent—that is, against those who, owing to their leisure, their vivid perceptions, quick sympathies, and unblunted sensibilities, can best appreciate what is beautiful, best profit by what is ennobling, and best reward, by innocence confirmed and noble enjoyments extended, the poet who has ever regarded *them* as his glory and his crown.

I have spoken, perhaps, at too great length of an evil which is yet but in an early stage amongst us.

But that evil is one which tends to advance. A busy age will need daily a noisier challenge; and a luxurious age, weary of honest pleasures, will crave stronger stimulants. Nor may a friendly appeal be without value to some of our younger writers, whose genius is capable of better things than they suspect, and who are tempted to err into by-paths, not by any natural preference for them, but by paradox and precipitancy, by vanity, or by a despair of coping with the classic masters on the broad highways of literature. The true aspirant can never have cause for despair. Fail who may, Poetry will never lack fit men through whom to send her message to man. The false prophets may prophesy deceits; but the true prophets will not cease to declare the vision or denounce the burthen. This volume records the name of several who in recent times have been true to their vocation; fortunate if thus, at least, it may help to attract some hearts to that true kingdom of poetry of which such writers are the representatives, and thus to make atonement in some measure for its own defects.

CONTENTS.

POEMS.

ODE I.

THE MUSIC OF THE FUTURE.

I.

HARK, hark that chime! The frosts are o'er!
  With song the birds force on the spring:
Thus, Ireland, sang thy bards of yore:—
  O younger bards, 'tis time to sing!
Your Country's smile that with the past
  Lay dead so long—that vanished smile—
Evoke it from the dark, and cast
  Its light around a tearful isle!

II.

Like severed locks that keep their light
  When all the stately frame is dust,
A Nation's songs preserve from blight
  A Nation's name, their sacred trust.

Temple and pyramid eterne
  May memorize her deeds of power;
But only from the songs we learn
  How throbbed her life-blood, hour by hour.

III.

Thrice blest the strain that brings to one
  Who weeps, by some Australian rill,
A worn out life far off begun,
  His Country's countenance beauteous still!
That 'mid Canadian wilds, or where
  Rich-feathered birds are void of song,
Wafts back, 'mid gusts of Irish air,
  Old wood-notes loved and lost so long!

IV.

Well might the Muse at times forsake
  Her Grecian hill, and sit where swerve
In lines like those of Hebé's neck,
  That wood-girt bay, yon meadow's curve,*
Watching the primrose clusters throw
  Their wan light o'er that ivied cave,
And airs by myrtles odored blow
  The apple blossom on the wave!

V.

Thrice blest the strain that, when the May
  Woos thus the young leaf from the bud,
When robins, thrushlike, shake the spray,
  And deepening purples tinge the flood,

* Foynes Island.

Kindles new worlds of love and truth,
  This world's lost Eden, still new-born,
In breast of Irish maid or youth,
  Reading beneath the Irish thorn:

VI.

That lures from over-heated strife
  Blinded ambition's tool; that o'er
The fields of unsabbatic life
  The church-bells of the past can pour;
Around the old oak lightning-scarred
  Can raise the virgin woods that rang
When, throned 'mid listening kerns, the bard
  Of Oisin and of Patrick sang.

VII.

Saturnian years return! Ere long
  Peace, justice-built, the Isle shall cheer:
Even now old sounds of ancient wrong
  At distance roll, and come not near:
Past is the iron age—the storms
  That lashed the worn cliff, shock on shock;
The bird in tempest cradled warms
  At last her wings upon the rock.

III.

How many a bard may lurk even now,
  Ireland, among thy noble poor!
To Truth their genius let them vow,
  And scorn the Syren's tinsel lure;

Faithful to illustrate God's word
  On Nature writ ; or re-revealing,
Through Nature, Christian lore transferred
  From faith to sight by songs heart-healing.

IX.

Fair land ! the skill was thine of old
  Upon the illumined scroll to trace
In heavenly blazon, blue or gold,
  The martyr's palm, the angel's face :
One day on every Muse's page
  Be thine a saintly light to fling,
And bathe the world's declining age
  Once more in its baptismal spring !

X.

Man sows : a Hand Divine must reap :
  The toil wins most that wins not praise :
Stones buried in oblivion's deep
  May help the destined pile to raise,
Foundations fix for pier or arch ;
  Above that spirit-bridge's span
To Faith's inviolate home may march,
  In God's good time, enfranchised man.

SONNET.

SARSFIELD AND CLARE.

SILENT they slumber in the unwholesome shade:
And why lament them? Virtue, too, can die:
Old wisdom labors in extremity;
And greatness stands aghast, and cries for aid
Full often: aye, and honor grows dismayed;
And all those eagle hopes, so pure and high,
Which soar aloft in youth's unclouded sky,
Drop dustward, self-subverted, self-betrayed.
Call it not joy to walk the immortal floor
Of this exulting earth, nor peace to lie
Where the thronged marbles awe the passer by:
True rest is this; the task, the mission o'er,
To bide God's time, and man's neglect to bear—
Hail, loyal Sarsfield! Hail, high-hearted Clare!

TO THE COUNT DE MONTALEMBERT

WITH A COPY OF "INISFAIL."

YOUR spirit walks in halls of light:
  On earth you breathe its sunnier climes:
How can an Irish muse invite
  Your fancy thus to sorrowing rhymes?

But you have fought the Church's fight!
  My Country's Cause and hers are one:
And every Cause that rests on Right
  Invokes Religion's bravest son.

ODE II.

CHRIST CHURCH CATHEDRAL, DUBLIN.

I.

Ho! ye that pace this way and that
  In all your Sunday bravery,
That ask "What news?" that laugh and chat
  Of Emperor, Pope, and slavery,
How name you yon cathedral hoar?
  Who built it? Who endowed it?
Why kneel the natives there no more
  While grooms and courtiers crowd it?

II.

One portion of its sacred trust
  That pile has ne'er discarded:
There Strongbow slumbers—tomb and dust
  By well-fed vergers guarded:
But those who clasp the faith *they* held,
  The invaders and the invaded,
Far off they kneel, a horde expelled,
  An alien tribe degraded.

III.

From roof to roof the wind may run,
  And shake the weeds close-shaven:
The javelin of the setting sun
  May glance from tower to raven;

They draw not nigh whose sires of old
  Upraised yon frowning steeple,
God's chimes who rolled at midnight cold
  Above a kneeling people!

IV.

A time there was when sheaf and blade,
  From ocean on to ocean
Confessed their Faith and tribute paid
  To ennoble their devotion:
Now on the wintry hills, scarce fed,
  The Church's flocks are driven
From Achill's Isle to Brandon's Head,
  Half shepherded, half shriven!

V

The Church ancestral sat in rags,
  A thorny garland wearing:
The sons of Ireland's wastes and crags
  For laws of man naught caring
Confessed, plain-voiced, whoe'er held sway,
  King, Parliament, Protector,
Their Faith—that Faith which mounts to-day,
  Above your Law-Church victor.

VI.

Law turned, to prop *that* Church, a wheel
  Of omnipresent torture
With swifter, subtler, steadier zeal
  Than lawless rage could nurture:

Keen scriveners—merchants, slow but fell—
  Half buccaneers, half hedgers—
Old Shylock's knife they whetted well
  Upon their dusty ledgers.*

VII.

Law banned the Book, the Trade, the Farm,
  To prop your State-Church fiction:
Law stretched o'er shipless seas an arm
  Of iron-bound restriction:
Law bribed the serf to hunt his Priest;
  Loosed wife and child from duty;
But the People were true:—*that* Church possessed
  Not them, but theirs, for booty.

VIII.

Statesmen, that oft—old thrones o'erturned—
  Of wrongs remote have ranted,
Has Pole, has Lombard ever mourned
  Or Faith or Church supplanted?
Take breath, avengers! Nearer claims
  Invoke your earlier favor;
The Tiber cleanse not till the Thames
  Sends up a healthier savor!

* The war of chicane succeeded to that of arms and of hostile statutes; and a regular series of operations was carried on, particularly from Chichester's time, in the ordinary courts of justice, and by special commissions and inquisitions, first, under pretence of tenures, and then of titles in the crown, for the purpose of the total extirpation of the interest of the natives in their own soil.—*Burke*, vol. vi. p. 336.

IX.

What voice is murmuring at mine ear,
  "We would, but are not able:
"Right sides with Interest;—yet we fear
  The zealot and the rabble."
Statesmen! Church-heat is seldom meet
  For undogmatic laymen;
Go, treat us Papists as you treat
  Your Budhist and your Brahmin!

X.

How soon shall Freedom spurn the weight
  Of centuries dead and gory?
How long the eighth Henry maculate
  Victoria's grace and glory?
Against our honor and the Queen's
  We deem this mockery:—end it!
Disloyal is the pen that screens,
  The bayonets that defend it!

XI.

Statesmen, look up! 'Tis Truth makes bold!
  Three centuries burst their prison;
From the sealed Tomb the stone is rolled:
  The Truth that slept hath risen.
Self caught in knots of serpent wiles
  Low lies the Equivocation;
And, o'er the ruin rising, smiles
  A liberated Nation!

SCOTLAND reveres her great Montrose,
  Scotland bewails her brave Dundee!
With Alfred's memory England glows:—
  What lethal hemlock freezes thee,

My country, that thy trophies rise
  To noteless men, or men ill-famed,
While they thy manlier destinies
  Who shaped, so long remain unnamed?

The Dutchman strides his steed new-gilt
  In thy chief city's stateliest way;
The Kings thy monarchy who built,
  Or died to save it, where are they?

Clontarf! That Prince who smote the Dane,
  That Prince who raised a realm laid low—
On thee what hath he? Benburb's plain
  No record bears of Owen Roe!

Forgotten now as Nial and Conn
  Are those twin stars of Yellow-Ford
Who freed Tyrconnell and Tyrone,
  Their country's altars who restored.

The man who feared no hireling's scoff,
  Thine Abdiel 'mid the apostate crew—
Grattan!—his statue stands far off;
  Berkeley wins late his laurels due.

Thy quarries have a barren womb,
  My country, or a monster birth!
Belong they, statue, pillar, tomb,
  To vice alone or modern worth?

Arise, and for thy proper weal
  Yield thy great Dead their honors late:
Those only understand who feel
  How self-disfranchised are the ingrate!

ODE III.

INDUSTRY.

I.

FREE children of a land set free,
  A land late bound in fetters,
Demand ye why your critic guest
  Scoffs oft in you his betters?
Nor race alone, nor creed to him
  Is stumbling-block, or scandal:
Your rags offend! he loathes in you
  Light purse and slipshod sandal.

II.

His Virtue builds on Self-Respect:
  Upon that clay foundation,
Nor rock nor sand, his trophies stand,
  The unit, and the nation.

Sad martyr of a finite Hope,
Nor seeks he, nor attains he
The all-heavenly prize. He toils for Earth;
But what he seeks that gains he.

III.

Grasp ye, with ampler aim, that good
His tragic creed o'erprizes:
With loftier Mind revere in him
The Will that energizes,
The strong right hand, the lion heart,
The industrial truth and valor:
When comes reverse he too can die,
But not in dirt and squalor.

IV.

The natural Virtues yield to those
Of heavenly birth affiance:
O ye so strong in Faith, be strong
In Truth and Self-Reliance!
Strength, Justice, Prudence, Self-constraint!—
Behold the four-square turret
From which—a triad spire—should rise
The Virtues of the Spirit!

V.

Upon your brows the sunrise breaks:
Then scorn the dirgeful ditty!
Never, be sure, the heart was strong
That dallied with self-pity.

Your Fathers' part was this—to bear—
  That plague they bore God stayeth:
Be yours to act! To manhood born,
  Be men! "Who worketh, prayeth."

VI.

Son of the sorrowing Isle, her eyes
  Arraign thee for unkindness!
Her shipless seas, her stagnant moors
  Accuse thy sloth or blindness.
Set free her greatness—sing to her,
  New harvests waving round thee,
"Thy son with golden robe hath girt,
  With golden crown hath crowned thee!"

VII.

Young maid, that bend'st above thy wheel,
  So pure, so meek, so simple,
The wool out-drawing as the smile
  Developes from the dimple,
Smile on! thou cloth'st thy country's feet,
  Those feet long bare and bleeding!
Smile on! thou send'st her Faith abroad
  With seemlier swiftness speeding!

VIII.

Advance, victorious Years! we land
  On solid shores and stable:
Recede, dim seas, and painted cloud
  Of legend and of fable!

The Heroic Age returns. Of old
  Men fought with spears and arrows :—
The sea-bank is the shield to-day :
  The true knight drains and harrows !

SONNET.

THE IRISH CONSTITUTION OF 1782.

NOBLES of Ireland ! they your work arraign
That won your victory ! Lightning-like the thrill
Of Liberty speeds on ! O land, be still !
Your patriots toiled, your vales rejoice in vain.
"Our Nation wears no more the servile stain !
Our People turns no more the conqueror's mill !"
Nation and People have ye none ! Your Will
Tyrannic knits anew the severed chain !*
Nobles of Ireland that would fain be free
Set free your Irish Helots ! From that hour
Nation and People equalled shall ye stand
With England, side to side, or brand to brand !
Boast not till then a Freedom void of Power :
A laughing Devil mocks such Liberty !

* The refusal of Parliamentary Reform, and of Catholic Emancipation, rendered the Irish Constitution of 1782 a nullity.

ODE IV.

IRELAND'S CHURCH RIGHT AND ULSTER'S "TENANT RIGHT;" OR, THE IRISH CATHOLIC TO THE PROTESTANT OF THE NORTH.

[The "Tenant Right," sometimes called the "Old Custom" of Ulster, founds its claims to Compensation, Fixity of Tenure, etc., not on Statutes, but on Common Law, Prescription, and Usage—principles of which the stronghold has ever been that traditional Religion denounced by those who make their especial boast of "Protestant Ulster."]

I.

STRONG Saxons of the dauntless North
  That jeer your Gaelic neighbors,
And cleave your dark, ice-muffled earth
  With earlier, sturdier labors,
Fierce Ulster's Tenants—scarce "at will"—
  That storm at "Landlord plunder,"
And swear that from the fields you till
  No force your hands shall sunder:—

II.

That toil in dream, that heap your hoards,
  That, sober-sad, or tipsy,
Scourge Mother Earth, great guano-Lords,
  Still crying, "More, old gipsy!"
And, like the Dutch, that "fished to shore"
  Through roaring waves the dry land,
Dig, delve, and through the trench's door,
  Drag up a second island:—

III.

Your world is Nature's world! 'Tis well:
Yet know there lives another,
A world of ampler plain and dell,
A kindlier, mightier Mother,
A loftier sphere the *soul* that feeds,
That sways with instincts finer
And satisfies from deeper meads
Necessities diviner.

IV.

Faith rules that world! 'Twas yours of old!
Aye, ages following ages
It teemed and reared the sacred mould
Of patriot saints and sages:
The Common Law of Christendom
The common Right protected:
The Church was heritage and home—
Themselves your sires "ejected."

V.

Truths richer than the Australian mine
They spurned on Power's pretences:
The Faith's celestial Discipline
Gave way to legal fences:
Amid a People's curses deep,
Or silent execration,
The men that readiest proved to creep
Were pitch-forked into station.

VI.

Scorners of Statute Law, who hail
  The ways traditionary,
What way found grace when Knox made pale
  The royal cheek of Mary?
When Luther, windier still than Knox,
  Proclaimed his Prophet mission,
And Nations veered like weather-cocks,
  Say, where was then "Tradition"?

VII.

Sirs, there are storms far off that die
  While near storms bruit and bluster!
You hear the falling roof-tree—I
  The violated cloister!
When winter blasts through fanes stripped bare
  First dashed, as still they dash on,
Was "Fixity of Tenure" there?
  Where then was "Compensation"?

VIII.

Maintainers of the "Old Custom," learn
  Old graves no more to trample!
Sad lyrists of the abandoned barn
  Restore the ravished temple!
Base not old rights on novel wrong!
  True Faith makes strong and true men:
Tyrone was true—Tyrconnel strong—
  Ye transient are, and new men!

IX.

None questions now King James' right,
  Or Ulster's "young Plantation:"
Time heals with lenient touch, like light,
  The scars of confiscation:
Old claims die out; new rights succeed;
  Men learn content, or feign it;
But Churches still live on, and bleed,
  Demand redress, and gain it.

X.

Ye know the weight of kine and corn,
  The price of beans and vetches;
Tell me what price a Nation torn
  In twain by faction fetches?
Be one! 'Tis vain to storm or 'plain,
  Till then, at "Landlord plunder:"
"Upper," till then, must rule and reign,
  And "Under" still be under.

January, 1855.

SONNET.

CHRISTIAN EDUCATION.

WHAT man can check the aspiring life that thrills
And glows through all this multitudinous wood;
That throbs in each minutest leaf and bud,
And, like a mighty wave ascending, fills
More high each day with flowers the encircling hills?—
From earth's maternal heart her ancient blood
Mounts to her breast in milk! her breath doth brood

O'er fields Spring-flushed round unimprisoned rills !
Such life is also in the breast of Man ;
Such blood is at the heart of every Nation,
Not to be chained by Statesman's frown or ban.
Hope and be strong : fear and be weak ! The seed
Is sown : be ours the prosperous growth to feed
With food, not poison—Christian Education !

ODE V.

THE BUILDING OF A COTTAGE.

I.

LAY foundations deep and strong
  On the rock, and not the sand :
Morn her sacred beam has flung
  O'er our ancient land.
And the children through the heather
  Beaming joy from frank bright eyes,
Dance along, and sing together
  Their loud ecstasies.
Children, hallowed song to-day !
Sing, aloud ; but, singing, pray !
Orphic measures, proudly swelling,
  Lifted cities in old time :
Build we now a humbler dwelling
  With a lowlier rhyme !
Unless God the work sustain,
Our toils are vain, and worse than vain :
Better to roam for aye, than rest
Under the impious shadow of a roof unblest !

II.

Mix the mortar o'er and o'er,
  Holy music singing:
Holy water o'er it pour,
  Flowers and tresses flinging:
Bless we now the earthen floor:
  May good Angels love it!
Bless we now the new-raised door:
  And that cell above it!
Holy cell, and holy shrine
For the Maid and Child divine!
Remember thou that see'st her bending
  O'er that babe upon her knee,
All Heaven is ever thus extending
  Its arms of love round thee!
Such thought thy step make light and gay
As yon elastic linden spray
On the smooth air nimbly dancing—
Thy spirits like the dew glittering thereon and
    glancing!

III.

Castles stern in pride o'er-gazing
  Subject leagues of wolds and woods;
Palace fronts their fretwork raising
  'Mid luxurious solitudes;
These, through clouds their heads uplifting,
  The lightning challenge and invoke:
His balance Power is ever shifting—
  The reed outlasts the oak.

Live, thou cottage! live and flourish,
Like a bank that spring showers nourish,
Bright with field-flowers self-renewing,
  Annual violets, dateless clover—
Eyes of flesh thy beauty viewing
  With a glance may pass it over;
But to eyes that wiser are
Thou glitterest like the morning star;
And o'er wise hearts thy beauty breathes
Such sweets as morn shall waft from those new-
    planted wreaths!

IV.

Our toils—not toils—are all but ended;
  The day has wandered by:
Her gleams the rising moon has blended
  With the azure of the sky:
Yet still the sunset lights are ranging
  On from mossy stem to stem;
Low winds, their odors vague exchanging,
  Chaunt day's requiem.
Upon the diamonded panes
The crimson falls with fainter stains.
More high in heavenward aspiration
  The gables shoot their mystic lines:
While now, supreme in grace as station,
  The tower-like chimney shines.
An altar stands that tower beneath:
Pure be its flame in life and death!
Now westward point the archéd porch—
Crown with a Cross the whole—our cot becomes
    a Church!

V.

Kings of the Earth ! too frail, too small
  This straw-roofed tenement for you ?
Then lo ! from Heaven my song shall call
  A statelier retinue !
They come, the twilight ether cheering,
(Not vain the suppliant song, not vain,)
Our earth on golden platform nearing :
  On us their crowns they rain !
Like Gods they stand, the portal
Lighting with looks immortal !
Faith, on her chalice gazing deep ;
  And Justice with uplifted scale ;
Meek Reverence ; pure, undreaming Sleep ;
  Valor in diamond mail !
There, Hope with vernal wreath ; hard by
Indulgent Love ; keen Purity ;
And Truth, with radiant forehead bare ;
And Mirth, whose ringing laughter triumphs o'er
    Despair.

VI.

Breathe low : stand mute in reverent trance !
  Those Potentates their mighty eyes
Have fixed ! Right well that piercing glance
  Roof, wall, and basement tries !
Foundations few that gaze can meet :
  Therefore the Virtues stay with few :
But where they once have fixed their seat,
  Her home Heaven fixes too !

They enter now with awful grace
Their dedicated dwelling place :
In tones majestical yet tender
  They chaunt their consecration hymn,
From jewelled breasts a sacred splendor
  Heaving through shadows dim.
The Rite is done : the seed is sown :
Leave, each his offering, and be gone !
Stay, ye for whom were raised these walls—
Possession God hath ta'en ; and now His guests
    He calls.

ODE VI.

THE FOUNDATION OF THE CATHOLIC UNIVERSITY.

I.

THE Land, how lies she cold and dead,
  When on her brow long since
Freedom its virtuous radiance shed,
  And drove the darkness thence ?
The child at her its stone may fling ;
The dragon-fly her cheek may sting—
"Ho ! murdered was she, or self-slain,
This bulk with blackness in the brain ?"

II.

'Tis past ! the Realm has learned its want :
  The Nation wills its work :
Her eastern skies with lustre pant,
  Vacant till now and murk :

She swears with heavenly Faith to join
The manly mind, the fixed design,
The mastering knowledge—public heart—
The nature crowned, not quenched by art.

III.

'Twas in a dolorous hour, 'twas then
  When Famine plagued our coast,
And Penal Law,* let loose again,
  Trod feebly like a ghost
The land he once had stamped in blood,
'Twas then her need we understood:
'Twas then her Genius from a cloud
Looked forth and cried to us aloud!

IV.

The People heard; and, far and wide,
  Like some long clarion blast,
By town, and plain, and mountain side
  The inspiring Mandate passed:
His children's crust the peasant shared
With him that brought the news, and bared
A hearth already blank to aid
That great emprize so long delayed.

V.

In Glendalough's green vale, and where
  The skylark sings o'er Lee,
Once more her domes shall Wisdom rear,
  And house the brave and free;

* The Ecclesiastical Titles Act, 1851.

From Cashel's rock, th' old Minster fane
Shall laugh in light o'er Thomond's plain;
Grey Arran pierce the sea-fog's gloom;
Kildare her vestal lamp relume.

VI.

Where Shannon sweeps by lost Athlone
  To Limerick's Castle walls
New college choirs the river's moan
  Shall tune at intervals;
By kingly Clonmacnoise, and Cong,
Fresh notes shall burst of olden song,
And by that wave-washed northern shore,
Whereon they toiled—those "Masters Four."

VII.

They toiled and toiled till sank the night:
  They toiled till aching morn
Through mist of breakers rose with light
  Uncertain and forlorn:
Their country's Present overcast,
They vowed thus much should live—her Past!
A beam o'er graves heroic shed,
And haunt with dreams the Oppressor's bed.

VIII.

Lo! where we stand, one day shall spread
  Cloisters like branching wood:
On the great Founder's sculptured head*
  Our Irish sunshine brood!

* Dr. Newman.

I see the fountains gem the grass;
Through murmuring courts the red gown pass;
Religion's pageant, and the vaunt
Of Learning mailed and militant.

IX.

I see, entombed in marble state,
  Roderick—O'More—Red Hugh;
The two crowned Mourners*—wise too late—
  Their tardy wisdom rue:
I see the Martyrs of old time;
The warriors hymned in Irish rhyme;
And Burke and Grattan, just in deed,
Though nurslings of an alien creed.

X.

The vision deepens: tower-cast shades
  With sunset longer grow:
High ranged round airy colonnades
  Fronting that western glow,
Lean out stone Patrons, veiled all day,
But vast at eve against the grey,
Like those great Hopes that o'er us shine
Distinctest in our life's decline.

XI.

'Tis night: the dusk arcades between
  Glimmers, O Derg, thy Lake!
The May moon o'er it trails serene
  Her silver-woven wake:

* Charles I. and James II.

What songs are those? Each boat has crossed
Half-way that radiance—and is lost,
Returning from the ivied pile
That hallows Iniscaltra's Isle.

XII.

The moon is set, and all is dark,
  Yet still those oars keep time:
The great clock shakes the courts, and hark,
  That many-steepled chime!
From college on to college roll
The peals o'er creek and woody knoll!—
My Country, *will* it! Fancy's store
Is rich: yet Faith can grant thee more!

SONNET.

WRITTEN IN CUMBERLAND, SEPT. 1860.

LAUREATES of Freedom o'er these hills sublime
That stride and ask, "What news? What tyrant's fall
Draws out to-day, in ruin musical,
The storm-stop of an else monotonous chime?"
The news is this—strange news in prose or rhyme—
They that redeemed this land, then Satan's thrall,
To Christ, were Ireland's sons! Iona's call
Your fathers spurned not in Faith's happy prime!*

* See the Count de Montalembert's noble work, "The Monks of the West."

To-day the sons of Ireland, far and near,
Amerced of altar, priest, and sacrifice,
Like the blind laboring horse or harnessed steer,
Sweat in your fields! I speak where none replies
Calm as a sceptic's smile still shines the sun:
The slowly sailing cloud sails slowly on!

ODE VII.

AFTER ONE OF THE FAMINE YEARS.

I.

THE golden dome, the Tyrian dye,
  And all that yearning ocean
Yields from red caves to glorify
  Ambition, or devotion—
I leave them—leave the bank of Seine,
  And those high towers that shade it,
To tread my native fields again,
  And muse on glories faded.

II.

The monumental city stands
  Around me in its vastness,
Girdling the spoils of all the lands
  In war's imperial fastness.
That stony scroll of every clime
  Some record boasts or sample;
Cathedral piles of oldest time,
  Huge arch and pillared temple.

III.

They charge across the field of Mars;
  The earth beneath them shaking
As breaks a rocket into stars
  The columned host is breaking:
It forms: it bursts:—new hosts succeed:
  They sweep the Tuileries under:
The thunder from the Invalides
  Answers the people's thunder.

IV.

Behold! my heart is otherwhere,
  My soul these pageants cheer not:
A cry from famished vales I hear,
  That cry which others hear not.
Sad eyes, as of a noontide ghost,
  Whose grief, not grace, first won me,
'Mid regal pomps ye haunt me most:—
  There most your power is on me.

V.

Last night, what time the convent shades,
  Far-stretched, the pavement darkened
Where rose but late the barricades
  Alone I stood, and hearkened;
Thy dove-note, O my country, thine,
  In long-drawn modulation,
Went by me, linked with words divine
  That stayed all earthly passion!

VI.

A man entranced, and yet scarce sad,
  Since then I see in vision
The scenes whereof my boyhood had
  Possession, not fruition.
Dark shadows sweep the landscape o'er,
  Each other still pursuing;
And lights from sinking suns once more
  Grow golden on the ruin.

VII.

Dark violet hills extend their chains
  Athwart the saffron even,
Pure purple stains not distant plains:
  And earth is mixed with heaven:
One cloud o'er half the sunset broods;
  And from its ragged edges
The wine-black shower descends like floods
  Down dashed from diamond ledges.

VIII.

Through rifted fanes the damp wind sweeps,
  Chanting a dreary psalter:
I see the bones that rise in heaps
  Where rose of old the altar;
Once more beside the blessed well
  I see the cripple kneeling:
I hear the broken chapel bell
  Where organs once were pealing.

IX.

I come, and bring not help, for God
  Withdraws not yet the chalice:
Still on your plains by martyrs trod
  And o'er your hills and valleys,
His name a suffering Saviour writes—
  Letters black-drawn, and graven
On lowly huts, and castled heights,
  Dim haunts of newt and raven.

X.

I come, and bring not song; for why
  Should grief from fancy borrow?
Why should a lute prolong a sigh,
  Sophisticating sorrow?
Dull opiates, down! To wind and wave,
  Lethean weeds I fling you:
Anacreontics of the grave,
  Not mine the heart to sing you!

XI.

I come the breath of sighs to breathe,
  Yet add not unto sighing
To kneel on graves, yet drop no wreath
  On those in darkness lying.
Sleep, chaste and true, a little while,
  The Saviour's flock, and Mary's:
And guard their reliques well, O Isle,
  Thou chief of reliquaries!

XII.

Blessed are they that claim no part
  In this world's pomp and laughter :
Blessed the pure ; the meek of heart :—
  Blest here ; more blest hereafter.
"Blessed the mourners." Earthly goods
  Are woes, the Master preaches :—
Embrace thy sad beatitudes,
  And recognize thy riches !

XIII.

And if, of every land the guest,
  Thine exile back returning
Finds still one land unlike the rest,
  Discrowned, disgraced, and mourning,
Give thanks ! Thy flowers, to yonder skies
  Transferred, pure airs are tasting ;
And, stone by stone, thy temples rise
  In regions everlasting.

XIV.

Sleep well, unsung by idle rhymes,
  Ye sufferers late and lowly ;
Ye saints and seers of earlier times,
  Sleep well in cloisters holy !
Above your bed the bramble bends,
  The yew tree and the alder :
Sleep well, O fathers, and O friends,
  And in your silence moulder !

SONNET.

TRUE AND FALSE LOVE OF FREEDOM.

THEY that for freedom feel not love but lust,
Irreverent, knowing not her spiritual claim,
And they, the votaries blind of windy fame,
And they who cry "I will because I must,"
They too that launch, screened by her shield august,
A bandit's shaft, some private mark their aim,
And they that make her sacred cause their game
From restlessness or spleen or sheer disgust
At duteous days ;--all these, the brood of night,
Diverse, by one black note detected stand,
Their scorn of every barrier raised by Right
To awe self-will. Howe'er by virtue bann'd,
By reason spurn'd, that act the moment needs
Licensed they deem ;—holy whate'er succeeds.

SONNET.

ROMANS, that lift to Liberty, your God,
Not vows, but swords, suppliants self-deified,
Betwixt her altars and your rock of pride
A stream there rolls fiercer than Alpine flood,
A fatal stream of murder'd Rossi's blood !*
For Liberty he lived ; and when he died,
Prisoner, that new Rienzi's corse beside,
The King, the Pontiff, and the Father stood !

* Such deeds as the murders of Rossi, of Lincoln, and of Thomas D'Arcy McGee remind us sadly of O'Connell's reiterated warning : "He who commits a crime is the *enemy of his country*."

What rite piacular from that impious deed
Hath cleansed your hands? Accuse not adverse stars
If guilt unwept achieve not virtue's meed.
Years heal not treason. All his sands old Time
Shakes down to keep unblurr'd those characters
Wherein are traced the calendars of crime.

ODE VIII.

THE DESOLATION OF THE WEST.

"Migravit Judah propter afflictionem."

I.

DAY after day, mile after mile,
I roamed a land that knew no smile
  With awe akin to dread:
The land remained: the hills were there:
The vales—but few remained to share
  That realm untenanted.

II.

Far-circling wastes, far-bending skies,
Clouds as at Nature's obsequies
  Slow trailing scarf and pall:—
In whistling winds on creaked the crane:
Grey lakes upstared from moor and plain
  Like eyes on God that call.

III.

Above the hoary main a bluff
Rose with unnumbered gables rough
  Beneath a sky of lead :
Nearer I drew : the tale was told !
Grim, roofless walls, and hearths long cold ;—
  The villagers were dead.

IV.

That race of old from Ulster driven
Once more—for ocean—or for heaven—
  Had rushed o'er Connaught's bound :
Void were the homes : the churchyards full :
Ten years had passed ; and many a skull
  Whitened the churchyard ground.

V.

Turn where I might, no blade of green
Diversified the tawny scene :
  Bushless the waste, and bare :
A dusky red the hills, as though
Some deluge ebbing years ago
  Had left but sea-weed there.

VI.

Dark red the vales : that single hue
O'er rotting swamps an aspect threw
  Monotonous yet grand :
Long feared—for centuries in decay—
Like a maimed lion there it lay,
  What once had been a Land.

VII.

Yet, day by day, as dropt the sun,
A furnace glare through vapors dun
  Illumed each mountain's head:
Old tower and keep their crowns of flame
That hour assumed; old years of shame
  Like fiends exorcised, fled.

VIII.

That hour, from sorrow's trance awaking,
My soul, like day from darkness breaking,
  .With might prophetic fired,
To those red hills and setting suns
Returned antiphonal response,
  As gleam by gleam expired.

IX.

And in my spirit grew and gathered
Knowledge that Ireland's worst was weathered,
  Her last dread penance paid;
Conviction that for earthly scath
In world-wide victories of her Faith
  Atonement should be made.

X.

Well rose to heaven the hosts who there
Upbuild the omnipotence of prayer
  O'er depths of vanquished grief!
Well breasted they the billows drear
A western Ireland who uprear
  Like some slow coral reef!

XI.

Thus musing, in remoter vision
Of God's "New Heavens" I had fruition,
  And saw, and inly burned:
And I beheld the multitude
Of those whose robes were washed in blood,
  Saw chains to sceptres turned!

XII.

And I saw Thrones, and Seers thereon
Judging, and Tribes like snow that shone,
  And diamond towers high-piled,
Towers of that City theirs at last,
Through tribulations who have passed,
  And theirs, the undefiled.

XIII.

A Land become a Monument!
Man works; but God's concealed intent
  Converts his worst to best.
The first of Altars was a Tomb—
Ireland! thy grave-stone shall become
  God's Altar in the West!

December 12, 1860.

ODE IX.

AGAINST FALSE FREEDOM.

I.

THE Nations have their parts assign'd:
The deaf one watches for the blind:
The blind for him that hears not hears:
Harmonious as the heavenly spheres
Despite their outward fret and jar
Their mutual ministrations are.
Some shine on history's earlier page;
Some prop the world's declining age:
One, one reserves her buried bloom
To flower–perchance on Winter's tomb.

II.

Greece, weak of Will but strong in Thought,
To Rome her arts and science brought:—
Rome, strong yet barbarous, gain'd from her
A staff, but, like Saint Christopher,
Knew not for whom his strength to use,
What yoke to bear, what master choose.
His neck the giant bent!—thereon
The Babe of Bethlehem sat! Anon
That staff his prop, that sacred freight
His guide, he waded through the strait,
And enter'd at a new world's gate.

III.

On that new stage were played once more
The parts in Greece rehearsed before :
Round fame's Olympic stadium vast
The new-born, emulous Nations raced ;
Now Spain, now France the headship won
(Unrisen the Russian Macedon):
But naught, O Ireland, like to thee
Hath been ! A Sphinx-like mystery,
At the world's feast thou sat'st death-pale ;
And blood-stains tinged thy sable veil.

IV.

Apostle, first, of worlds unseen!
For ages, then, deject and mean :—
Be sure, sad land, a concord lay
Between thy darkness and thy day!
Thy hand, had temporal gifts been thine,
Had lost, perchance, the things divine.
Truth's witness sole ! The insurgent North
Gave way when falsehood's flood went forth
On the scarr'd coasts deform'd and cleft
Thou, like the Church's Rock, wert left !

V.

That Tudor tyranny which stood
'Mid wrecks of Faith, was quench'd in blood
When Charles, its child and victim, lay
The Rebel-Prophet's bleeding prey.

Once more the destined wheel goes round!
Heads royal long are half discrown'd:
Ancestral rights decline and die:—
Thus Despotism and Anarchy
Alternate each the other chase,
Twin Bacchantes wreathed around one vase.

VI.

The future sleeps in night: but thou
O Island of the branded brow,
Her flatteries scorn who rear'd by Seine
Fraternity's ensanguined reign,
And for a sceptre twice abhorr'd
Twice welcomed the Cesarian sword—
Thy past, thy hopes, are thine alone!
Though crush'd around thee and o'erthrown,
The majesty of civil might
The hierarchy of social right
Firm state in thee for ever hold!
Religion was their life and mould.

VII.

The vulgar, dog-like eye can see
Only the ignobler traits in thee;
Quaint follies of a fleeting time;
Dark reliques of the oppressor's crime.
The Seer—what sees he? What the West
Has ne'er except in thee possess'd;
The childlike Faith, the Will like fate,
And that Theistic Instinct great
New worlds that summons from the abyss
"The balance to redress of this."

VIII.

Wait thou the end; and spurn the while
False Freedom's meretricious smile!
Stoop not thy front to anticipate
A triumph certain! Watch and wait!
The schismatic, by birth akin
To Socialist and Jacobin,
Will claim, when shift the scales of power,
His natural place. Be thine that hour
With good his evil to requite;
To save him in his own despite;
And backward scare the brood of night!

SONNET.

THE ECCLESIASTICAL TITLES ACT.

THE statesmen of this day I deem a tribe
That dwarf-like strut, a pageant on a stage
Theirs but in pomp and outward equipage,
Ruled inly by the herd, or hireling scribe.
They have this skill, the dreaded Power to bribe:
This courage, war upon the weak to wage:
To turn from self a Nation's ignorant rage:
To unstaunch old wounds with edict or with jibe.
Ireland! The unwise one saw thee in the dust,
Crowned with eclipse, and garmented with night,

And in his heart he said, "For her no day!"
But thou long since hadst placed in God thy trust,
And knew'st that in the under-world, all light,
Thy sun moved eastward. Watch! that East
grows grey!

ODE X.

AN IRISH "GOD SAVE THE QUEEN."

I.

God save the Queen! A widowed land
May bless a Widow keeping
Beside a grave her faithful stand,
Long watching, and late weeping:
Well versed in woes, that land may pray,
"While the great night draws nearer,
Lady, may stars unseen by day
For thee grow clear and clearer!'

II.

God save the Queen, and drive far off
Each whisperer—clown or noble—
That dares her People's Faith to scoff,
Her People's peace to trouble;
Rebuke bad laws that bar with gloom
Her empire's rifted centre,
And freeze its Eden to a tomb—
A many-centuried winter.

III.

God save the Queen! His Strength, His Right
  Keep well:—they long have kept her!
All majesties of Love and Might
  Like eaglets haunt her sceptre!
Be hers a Realm for virtue praised,
  Not wealth alone; a Nation
Aloft in all its Orders raised,
  With just and wise gradation.

IV.

God save the Queen! Let flatterers run
  To hail the rising splendor:
To *her* more dear the sinking sun,
  That Island true and tender!
She that fought last for Charles—for James—
  Will yield more generous duty
To Virtue's grace, and Sorrow's claims
  Than all thy new-crowned beauty!

V.

God save the Queen! The land that weeps
  Her children fled or flying,
That, age by age, on carnage heaps
  Beheld her princes lying,
That land, O royal Mother, prays,
  Thy children round thee pressing,
May crown thy dimmed, autumnal days,
  With glory and with blessing.

VI.

God save the Queen! From Chiefs of yore
Who left for Alba's mountains
Dalriad Ireland's northern shore,*
Her life-blood tracks its fountains:—
Ring out, strong voices, and be glad!
Make answer, tower and steeple!
God save the Queen! But let her add
Her prayer, "God save my People!"

PROLOGUE TO CARDINAL WISEMAN'S "HIDDEN GEM."

FOUNDED ON THE LEGEND OF ST. ALEXIUS, AND ACTED BY THE PUPILS AT THE CISTERCIAN ABBEY OF MOUNT MELLERAY, WATERFORD, ON THE FEAST OF THE TRANSFIGURATION, 1863.

WHAT man is this, the poorest of the poor,
Who stands in rags beside a princely door?
Sea-surf, and winds that pipe o'er moorlands bleak
Have made a rude acquaintance with his cheek;
But from his eye looks forth a quenchless light,
Radiance of realms eterne and infinite!
He asks a boon:—like one of royal race,
That boon demands—the *lowliest* resting place!

* See Sir Walter Scott's History of Scotland.

Round him rich marbles gleam, proud bondsmen
laugh
Like idiots gibbering o'er an epitaph:
To him a palace yields a Hermit's grot:
He to his own has come; they know him not.

What man is this that from his pallet bed
Sends up that awful mandate from the Dead?
O'er the cold corse who weeps? No more beguiled
The Father's heart turns, clamorous, to the Child:
Great Rome is troubled: mute on either hand
A Pontiff, and an Emperor wondering stand:
But Truth shines clear at last through transient gloom;
And Love, Truth's martyr, conquers from the tomb.

Lo! this is he at God's command who spurned
The earth, and heaven's high lore through suffering
learned.
Fortune, that, queen-like, glittered at his side,
He fled, and Poverty embraced—his Bride.
Good Deeds his children were; Wisdom his crown;
His sceptre this, to rule one heart—his own.
Man's Race had moulted long its spirit-wings
Through gross and lavish use of lawful things,
Not less than things unlawful. As a sign
God raised this Witness for the things divine.
A greater light puts out, or dims, a less:
He fled from loves that innocently bless
In Heavenly Love's severe, yet sweet excess.

High is our theme! not Passion's feverish strife;
Not Fate at noon eclipsing Love and Life;
But Strength heroic by a path austere
Ascending darkly to a loftier sphere.
For once religious is a classic Muse:
But who could here a Pagan hero choose,
Here, where in regions desert, late, and lorn
Once more the Angelus attunes the morn,
Where Compline-Psalm, and Nocturn's wakeful Rite
Close and unclose with song the gates of night,
Where Benedict and Bernard's long-linked line
Respond to anthems from Mount Aventine?*
O Thou, our Nurse! High Mother of our spirits!
Strong Prophet of that kingdom Faith inherits;
With garb ascetic and perpetual Lent
A Baptist, crying to the World, "Repent!"
Yet inly clad with sun-like splendor! We
That beam transfiguring recognize in thee!
Our Theme art *thou!* The legend comes from
Rome:—
We found Alexius in our Irish home!

* The Church of St. Alexius stands on the Aventine.

TO BURNS'S "HIGHLAND MARY."

I.

O LOVED by him whom Scotland loves,
  Long loved, and honored duly
By all who love the bard who sang
  So sweetly and so truly !
In cultured dales his song prevails ;
  Thrills o'er the eagle's aëry—
Who, who that strain has caught, nor sighed
  For Burns's "Highland Mary" ?

II.

His golden hours of youth were thine ;
  Those hours whose flight is fleetest :
Of all his songs to thee he gave
  The freshest and the sweetest.
Ere ripe the fruit, one branch he brake,
  Snow-white with bursting blossom ;
And shook its dews, its incense shook,
  Above thy brow and bosom !

III.

And when his Spring, alas, how soon !
  Had been by care subverted,
His Summer, like a god repulsed,
  Had from his gates departed

Beneath the evening star, once more,
  Star of his morn and even!
To thee his suppliant hands he spread,
  And hailed his love "in heaven."

IV.

And if his being in "a waste
  Of shame" too oft was squandered,
And if too oft his feet ill-starred
  In ways erroneous wandered,
Ah! still his spirit's spirit bathed
  In purity eternal;
And all fair things through thee retained
  For him their aspect vernal!

V.

Nor less that tenderness remained
  Thy favoring love implanted;
Compunctious pity, yearnings vague
  For love to earth not granted;
Reserve with freedom, female grace
  Well matched with manly vigor
In songs where fancy twined her wreaths
  Round judgment's stalwart rigor.

VI.

A mute but strong appeal was made
  To him by feeblest creatures:
In his large heart had each a part
  That part had found in Nature's:

The wildered sheep, sagacious dog,
  Old horse reduced and crazy,
The field-mouse by the plough upturned,
  And violated daisy.

VII.

In him there burned that passionate glow,
  All Nature's soul and savor,
Which gives its hue to every flower,
  To every fruit its flavor:
Nor less the kindred power he felt;
  That love of all things human
Whereof the fiery centre is
  The love man bears to woman.

VIII.

He sang the dignity of man,
  Sang woman's grace and goodness;
Passed by the world's half-truths, her lies
  Pierced through with lance-like shrewdness.
Upon life's broad highways he stood,
  And aped nor Greek nor Roman;
But snatched from heaven Promethean fire
  To glorify things common.

IX.

He sang of youth, he sang of age,
  Their joys, their griefs, their labors;
Felt with, not for, the people, hailed
  All Scotland's sons his neighbors:

And therefore all repeat his verse—
  Hot youth, or graybeard steady,
The boatman on Loch Etive's wave,
  The shepherd on Ben Ledi.

X.

He sang from love of song; his name
  Dunedin's cliff resounded:—
He left her, faithful to a fame
  On truth and nature founded.
He sought true fame, not loud acclaim;
  Himself and Time he trusted:
For laurels crackling in the flame
  His fine ear never lusted!

XI.

He loved, and reason had to love,
  The illustrious land that bore him:
Where'er he went, like heaven's broad tent
  A star-bright Past hung o'er him.
Each isle had fenced a saint recluse,
  Each tower a hero dying;
Down every mountain-gorge had rolled
  The flood of foemen flying.

XII.

From age to age that land has paid
  No alien throne submission;
For feudal faith had been her Law,
  And Freedom her Tradition.

Where frowned the rocks had Freedom smiled,
  Sung, 'mid the shrill wind's whistle—
So England prized her garden Rose,
  But Scotland loved her Thistle.

XIII.

Fair field alone the brave demand,
  And Scotland ne'er had lost it:
And honest prove the hate and love
  To objects meet adjusted.
Her will and way had ne'er been crossed
  In fatal contradiction;
Nor loyalty to treason soured,
  Nor faith abused with fiction.

XIV.

Honor to Scotland and to Burns!
  In him she stands collected:
A thousand streams one river make—
  Thus Genius, heaven-directed,
Conjoins all separate veins of power,
  In one great soul-creation;
Thus blends a million men to make
  The Poet of the nation!

XV.

Be green for aye, green bank and brae
  Around Montgomery's Castle!
Blow there, ye earliest flowers, and there,
  Ye sweetest song-birds, nestle!

For there was ta'en that last farewell
  In hope, indulged how blindly ;
And there was given that long, last gaze
  "That dwelt" on him "sae kindly."

XVI.

No word of thine recorded stands ;
  Few words that hour were spoken :
Two Bibles were exchanged that hour,
  And some slight love-gift broken :
And there thy cold, faint hands he pressed,
  Thy head, by dew-drops misted :
And kisses, ill-resisted first,
  At last were unresisted.

XVII.

Ah ! cease—she died. He, too, is dead.
  Of all her girlish graces
Perhaps one severed tress remains :
  The rest stern Time effaces—
Dust lost in dust ! Not so : a bloom
  Is hers that ne'er can wither ;
And in that lay which lives for aye
  The twain live on together !

SONNET.

TO CHARLES ELIOT NORTON, ON READING HIS "VITA NUOVA" OF DANTE.

NORTON! I would that oft in years to come
The destined bard of that brave land* of thine,
Sole-seated 'neath the tempest-roughen'd pine,
In boyhood's spring when genius first doth plume
Her wing, 'mid forest scents and insects' hum
And murmurs from the far sea crystalline,
May smell *this* blossom from the Tuscan vine,
May hear *this* voice from antique Christendom!
For thus from love and purity and might
Shall he receive his armor, and forth fare
Worthy to range in song that country's knight
Who early burst the chains weak nations bear,
Weeping. 'Mid trumpet-blasts and standards torn
To manhood, with loud cries, thy land was born!

March 28, 1860.

SONNET.

LET me be near thee, and I will not touch
Thine hand, or grieve thee with reproach or praise,
Or look into thine eyes. Is this too much?
Sweet Lady, say not so, for I would gaze

* America.

On thee for ever. Be but what thou art,
A Beauty shrined within a silver haze;
And in the silence let me fill my heart
With memories calmly stored for wintry days.
O Lady, there is sorrow here below!
And gladness seldom comes, and cannot last:
Thou art all Summer: thou wilt never know
The cold and cloudy skies which I forecast:
Deny not thou long years of future woe
Their comfort sad and sole—a happy Past.

SONNET.

HAPPY are they who kiss thee, morn and even,
Parting the hair upon thy forehead white:
For them the sky is bluer and more bright,
And purer their thanksgivings rise to Heaven:
Happy are they to whom thy songs are given:
Happy are they on whom thy hands alight:
And happiest they for whom thy prayers at night
In tender piety so oft have striven.
Away with vain regrets and selfish sighs—
Even I, dear friend, am lonely, not unblest:
Permitted sometimes on that head to gaze,
Or feel the light of those consoling eyes—
If but a moment on my cheek it stays
I know that gentle beam from all the rest!

SONNET.

PAUSE, lovely Lady, pause: with downward eye
Regard this humble tomb awhile, and read
The name of him who loved you well, now freed
From pains of love—Ah, mournful liberty!
Sigh forth, too late, an unavailing sigh;
And, if thy spirit be to pity moved,
Pray that a ceaseless dream of her he loved
Abide upon him everlastingly.
Stay, lovely Lady, stay; oh! stay for hours:
I feel thy tear-drops falling one by one:
Yet do not stay, for grief and shame it were
That tears should fall so fast from eyes so fair,
And feet that scarcely bend the meadow flowers
Linger so long upon the chilling stone.

SONNET.

SILENCE and Sleep, and Midnight's softest gloom
Consoling friends of fast declining years;
Benign assuagers of unfruitful tears;
Soft-footed heralds of the wished-for tomb!
Go to your master Death, the Monarch whom
Ye serve; whose majesty your grace endears;
And in the awful hollows of his ears
Murmur, for ever murmur, "Come, oh! come."
Virginal rites have I performed full long,
And all observance worthy of a bride:

Then wherefore, Death, dost thou to me this wrong,
So long estranged to linger from my side?
Am I not thine? Oh! breathe upon my eyes
A gentle answer, Death, from thine Elysian skies!

A FAREWELL TO NAPLES.

I.

A GLORIOUS amphitheatre whose girth
Exceeds three-fold th' horizons of the north,
Mixing our pleasure in a goblet wide,
With hard, firm rim through clear air far-descried;
Illumined mountains, on whose heavenly slopes
Quick, busy shades rehearse, while Phœbus drops,
Dramatic parts in scenic mysteries;
Far-shadowing islands, and exulting seas,
With cities girt, that catch, till day is done,
Successive glances from the circling sun,
And cast a snowy gleam across the blue;
A gulf that, to its lake-like softness true,
Reveres the stillness of the Syren's cell,
Yet knows the ocean's roll, and loves it well;
A gulf where Zephyr oft, with noontide heat
Oppressed, descends to bathe his sacred feet,
And, at the first cold touch at once reviving,
Sinks to the wings in joy, before him driving
A feathery foam into the lemon groves;
Evasive, zone-like sands and secret coves;

Translucent waves that, heaved with motion slow
On fanes submerged a brighter gleam bestow;
Fair hamlets, streets with odorous myrtles spread,
Bruised by processions grave with soundless tread,
That leave (the Duomo entered) on the mind
A pomp confused, and music on the wind;
Smooth, mounded banks like inland coasts and capes,
That take from seas extinct their sinuous shapes,
And girdle plains whose growths, fire-fed below,
Without the bending laborer burst and blow;
A light Olympian and an air divine—
Naples! if these are blessings, they are thine.

II.

Thy sands we paced in sunlight and soft gloom;
From Tasso's birthplace roamed to Virgil's tomb:
Baia! thy haunts we trod, and glimmering caves
Whose ambushed ardors pant o'er vine-decked waves
Thy cliffs we coasted, loitered in thy creeks,
O shaggy island* with the five grey peaks!
Explored thy grotto, scaled thy fortress, where
Thy dark-eyed maids trip down the rocky stair,
With glance cast backward, laugh of playful scorn,
And cheek carnationed with the lights of morn.
The hills Lactarean lodged us in their breast:
Shadowy Sorrento to her spicy nest
Called us from far with gales embalmed, yet pure;
Her orange brakes we pierced, and ranged her rifts
obscure.

* Capri.

Breathless along Pompeii's streets we strayed
By songless fount, mosaic undecayed,
Voluptuous tomb, still forum, painted hall,
Where wreathed Bacchantès float on every wall,
Where Ariadne, by the purple deep,
Hears not those panting sails, but smiles in sleep,
Where yet Silenus grasps the woodland cup,
And buried Pleasure from its grave looks up.
Lastly, the great Vesuvian steep we clomb;
Then, Naples! made once more with thee our home.
We leave thee now: but first, with just review,
We cast the account, and strike the balance true:
And thus, as forth we fare, we take our last adieu.

III.

From her whom genius never yet inspired,
Nor virtue raised, nor pulse heroic fired;
From her who, in the grand historic page,
Maintains one barren blank from age to age;
From her, with insect life and insect buzz,
Who, evermore unresting, nothing does;
From her who, with the future and the past
No commerce holds, no structure rears to last;
From streets where spies and jesters, side by side,
Range the rank markets, and their gains divide;
Where Faith in Art, and Art in sense is lost,
And toys and gewgaws form a nation's boast;
Where Passion, from Affection's bond cut loose,
Revels in orgies of its own abuse;
And Appetite, from Passion's portals thrust,
Creeps on its belly to its grave of dust;

Where Vice her mask disdains, where Fraud is loud,
And naught but Wisdom dumb and Justice cowed;—
Lastly, from her who planted here unawed,
'Mid heaven-topped hills, and waters bright and broad,
From these but nerves more swift to err hath gained,
And the dread stamp of sanctities profaned,
And, girt not less with ruin, lives to show
That worse than wasted weal is wasted woe,—
We part, forth issuing through her closing gate
With unreverting faces, not ingrate.

1844.

PSYCHE,

OR, AN OLD POET'S LOVE.

I.

O ORIENT Isle that gave her birth!
  O Delos of a holier sea!
O casket of uncounted worth!
  How dear thou art to Love and me!

Thy whispering woods in some soft dell
  Now charmed, now broke the Infant's rest;
Thy vales the wild-flower cherished well
  Predestined for the Virgin's breast.

May airs salubrious, gusts of balm,
  On all thy shores incumbent, blow
Thy billow from the glassy calm,
  And fringe thy myrtles with sea-snow!

My Psyche's lips thy zephyrs breathe;
  My Psyche's feet thy pastures tread:—
O Isle of isles around me wreathe
  Thine asphodels when I am dead!

II.

How blue were Ariadne's eyes
  When, from the sea's horizon line,
At eve she raised them on the skies;
  My Psyche, bluer far are thine.

How pallid, snatched from falling flowers,
  The cheek averse of Proserpine,
Unshadowed yet by Stygian bowers;
  My Psyche, paler far is thine.

Yet thee no lover e'er forsook;
  No tyrant urged with love unkind:
Thy joy the ungentle cannot brook;
  Thy light would strike the unworthy blind.

A golden flame invests thy tresses:
  An azure flame invests thine eyes:
And well that wingless form expresses
  Communion with relinquished skies.

Forbear, O breezes of the West,
  To waft her to her native bourne;
For heavenly, by her feet impressed,
  Becomes our ancient earth outworn.

On Psyche's life our beings hang:
  In Psyche life and love are one:—
My Psyche glanced at me and sang,
  "Perhaps to-morrow I am gone!"

III.

PSYCHE'S BATH.

O stream beloved! O stream unknown!
  In which my love has bathed!
Be still thy fount unvexed with floods,
  Thy marge by heats unscathed.

How oft her white hand tempted thine!
  How oft, by fears delayed,
Ere yet her light had filled thy depth,
  With thee her shadow played!

Thy purity encompassed hers;
  Thy crystal cased my pearl;
Of founts, the fairest fount embraced
  Of girls, the loveliest girl.

May still thy lilies round thee wave,
  As shaken by a sigh!
Thy violets, blooming where she gazed,
  Bloom first and latest die!

May better bards, when I am gone,
  Like birds salute thy bower;
And each that sings thee grow in heart
  A virgin from that hour.

IV.

PSYCHE'S STUDY.

The low sun smote the topmost rocks,
  Ascending o'er the eastern sea:
Backward my Psyche waved her locks;
  And held her book upon her knee.

No brake was near, no flower, no bird,
  No music but the ocean wave,
That with complacent murmur stirred
  The echoes of a neighboring cave.

Absorbed my Psyche sat, her face
  Reflecting Plato's sun-like soul;
And seemed in every word to trace
  The pent-up spirit of the whole.

Absorbed she sat in breathless mood,
  Unmoved as kneeler at a shrine,
Save one slight finger that pursued
  The meaning on from line to line.

As some white flower in forest nook
  Bends o'er its own face in a well,
So seemed the virgin in that book
  Her soul, unread before, to spell.

Sudden, a crimson butterfly
  On that illumined page alit:—
My Psyche flung the volume by,
  And sister-like, gave chase to it!

V.

PSYCHE SINGING.

Between the green hill and the cloud
  The skylark loosed his silver chain
Of rapturous music, clear and loud—
  My Psyche answered back the strain.

A glory raced along the sky;
  She sang, and all dark things grew plain;
Hope, starlike, shone; and Memory
  Flashed like a cypress gemmed with rain.

The noble warfare recommenced;
  Once more that skylark's challenge rang:
Once more with him my Psyche fenced;
  At last the twain commingled sang.

Then first I learned the skylark's lore;
  Then first the words he sang I knew:
My soul with transport flooded o'er
  As breeze-borne gossamer with dew.

VI.

"Can Love be just? can Hope be wise?
  Can Youth renew his honors dead?"
On me my Psyche turned her eyes;
  And all my great resolves were fled.

Psyche, I said, when thou art nigh
  Transpicuous grow the mists of years:
I cannot ever wholly die
  If on my grave should drop thy tears.

Nor thine a part in mortal hours:
  Thy flower nor Autumn knows, nor May:
Thou bendest from sidereal bowers
  A shape supernal, bright for aye.

Though I be nothing, yet the best
  To thee no gift of price could give :—
Fall then in radiance on my breast
  And in thy blessing bid me live !

VII.

Pure lip coralline, slightly stirred ;
  Thus stir ; but speak not ! Love can see
On you the syllables unheard
  Which are his only melody.

Pure, drooping lids, dark lashes wet
  With that unhoped-for, trembling tear,
Thus droop, thus meet ; nor give me yet
  The eyes that I desire, yet fear.

Hands lightly clasped on meekest knee ;
  All-beauteous head, as by a spell
Bent forward ; loveliest form, to me
  A lovely soul made visible ;

Speak not ! move not ! More tender grows
  The heart, long musing. Night may plead,
Perhaps, my part, and, at its close,
  The morning bring me light indeed.

VIII.

She leaves us: many a gentler breast
Will mourn our common loss like me:
The babe her hands, her voice caressed,
The lamb that couched beside her knee.

The touch thou lov'st—the robe's far gleam—
Thou shalt not find, thou dark-eyed fawn!
Thy light is lost, exultant stream:
Dim woods, your sweetness is withdrawn.

Descend, dark heavens, and flood with rain
Their crimson roofs; their silence rout:
Their vapor-laden branches strain;
And force the smothered sadness out!

That so the ascended moon, when breaks
The cloud, may light once more a scene
Fair as some cheek that suffering makes
Only more tearfully serene:—

That so the vale she loved may look
Calm as some cloister roofed with snows,
Wherein, unseen, in shadowy nook,
A buried Vestal finds repose.

IX.

What art thou? If thou livest, I know
  That thou art good, and true, and fair:
But there are dreams that whisper low,
  "Thou dream'st! thy passion paints the air.

"Grief sat upon thy heart for years:—
  That heart, by light bewildered now,
All that it missed beholds through tears
  Throned on a single, beaming brow.

"Or else thy Fancy, tired of dust,
  Unsphered a Spirit. Self-enthralled,
It worships now, because it must,
  An Idol pride at first enstalled.

"Or else the pathos of the past
  Above thy present moves in power;
And o'er thy dusty day hath cast
  This dew-drop from its matin hour.

"In her thou lov'st the times gone by,
  In her the joys possessed, not missed:
It was not Hope, but Memory
  Thy dreaming lids that bent and kissed!

"In her the dewy lawns forlorn
  Thou lov'st; the gleams along them flung;
The witcheries of the awakening morn;
  The echo of its latest song.

"Thou tread'st once more Castalia's brink:
  Far down, thy youth finds rest from trouble;
And thou that saw'st it slowly sink
  Dost watch its latest breaking bubble."

ODE.

THE ASCENT OF THE APENNINES.

I.

I MOVE through a land like a land of dream,
Where the things that are, and that shall be, seem
Wov'n into one by a hand of air,
And the Good looks piercingly down through the
    Fair!
No form material is here unmated,
  Here blows no bud, no scent can rise,
No song ring forth, unconsecrated
  To a meaning or model in Paradise!
Fallen, like man, is elsewhere the earth;
Human, at best, in her sadness and mirth;
Or if she aspires after something greater,
  Lifting her hands from her native dust,
  In God she beholds but the wise, the just;
The Saviour she sees not in the Creator:
But here, like children of saints who learn
  The things above ere the things below,
Who choirs angelic in clouds discern
  Ere the butterfly's wing from the moth's they
    know,

True Nature as ashes all beauty reckons
  That claims not hereafter some happier birth
She calls from the height to the depth ; she beckons
  From the nomad waste to a heavenly hearth :
"The curse is cancelled," she cries ; "thou dreamer,
Earth felt the tread of the great Redeemer !"

II.

Ye who ascend with reverent foot
  The warm vale's rocky stairs,
Though lip be mute, in heart salute
  With praises and with prayers
The noble hands, now dust, that reared
  Long ages since on crag or sward
Those Stations from their cells revered
  Still preaching of the Lord !
Ah ! unseductive here the breath
  Of the vine-bud that blows in the breast of morn ;
That orange bower, yon jasmine wreath,
  Hide not the crown of thorn !
Here none can bless the spring, and drink
  The waters from the dark that burst,
Nor see the sponge and the reed, and think
  Of the Three Hours' unquenched thirst.
The Tender, the Beauteous receives its comment
  From a truth transcendent, a life divine ;
And the coin flung loose of the passing moment
  Is stamped with Eternity's sign !

III.

Alas for the wilder'd days of yore
When Nature lay vassal to pagan lore!
Baia—what was she? A sorceress still
To brute transforming the human will!
Nor pine could whisper, nor breeze could move
  But a breath infected ran o'er the blood
Like gales that whiten the aspen grove
  Or gusts that darken the flood.
Along the ocean's gleaming level
The beauteous base ones held their revel,
Dances on the sea-sand knitting,
  With shouts the sleeping shepherd scaring,
Like Oreads o'er the hill-side flitting,
  Like Mænads thyrsus-bearing.
The Siren sang from the moonlit bay,
  The Siren sang from the redd'ning lawn,
Until in the crystal cup of day
  Lay melted the pearl of dawn.
Unspiritual intelligence
Changed Nature's fane to a hall of sense,
That rings with the upstart spoiler's jest,
And the beakers clash'd by the drunken guest!

IV.

  Hark to that convent bell!
  False pagan world, farewell;
From cliff to cliff the challenge vaults rebounded!

Echo, her wanderings done,
Heart-peace at last hath won,
The rest of love on Faith not Fancy founded;
"By the parch'd fountain let the pale flower die,"
She sings, "True love, true joy, triumphant reign
on high!"

V.

The plains recede; the olives dwindle;
The chestnut slopes fall far behind;
The skirts of the billowy pine-woods kindle
In the evening lights and wind.
Not here we sigh for the Alpine glory
Of peak primeval and death-pale snow;
For the cold grey green, and the glacier hoary,
Or blue caves that yawn below.
The landscape here is mature and mellow;
Fruit-like, not flower-like:—hills embrown'd;
Ridges of purple and ledges of yellow
From red stream to rock church-crown'd:
'Tis a region of mystery, hush'd and sainted:
Serene as the visions of artists old
When the thoughts of Dante his Giotto painted:—
The summit is reach'd! Behold!
Like a sky condensed lies the lake far down;
Its curves like the orbit of some fair planet;
A fire-wreath falls on the cliffs that frown
Above it—dark walls of granite;
The hill-sides with homesteads and hamlets glow;
With snowy villages zoned below:

Down drops by the island's woody shores
The banner'd barge with the rhythmic oars.
No solitude here, no desert cheerless
  Is needed pure thoughts or hearts to guard;
'Tis a populous solitude, festal, fearless,
  For men of good-will prepared.
The hermit may hide in the wood, but o'er it
  All day the happy chimes are rolled:
The black crag wooes the cloud, but before it
  The procession winds on white-stoled.
Farewell, O Nature! None meets thee here
But his heart goes up to a happier sphere!
The radiance around him spread forgetting
  That City he sees on whose golden walls
No light of a rising sun, or setting,
  Of moon or of planet falls,
For the Lamb alone is the light thereof—
The City of Truth, the Kingdom of Love!

VI.

There shall the features worn and wasted
  Let fall the sullen mask of years:
There shall that fruit at last be tasted
  Whose seed was sown in tears:
There shall that amaranth bloom for ever
  Whose blighted blossom droop'd erewhile
  In this dim valley of exile,
And by the Babylonian river.
The loved and lost once more shall meet us;
Joys that never were ours shall greet us;

Delights for the love of the Cross foregone
Fullfaced salute us, ashamed of none.
Heroes unnamed the storm that weathered
  There shall sceptred stand and crown'd ;
Apostles the wilder'd flocks that gather'd
  Sit with the nations round.
There, heavenly sweets from the earthly bitter
  Shall rise like odor from herbs down-trod ;
There, tears of the past like gems shall glitter
  On the trees that gladden the mount of God.
The deeds of the righteous, on earth despised,
By the lightning of God immortalized
Shall crown like statues the walls sublime
  Of all the illuminate, mystic City,
Memorial emblems that conquer Time,
  Yet tell his tale. That Pity
Which gave the lost one strength to speak,
  That Love in guise angelic stooping
O'er the grey old head, or the furrow'd cheek,
  Or the neck depress'd and drooping,
Shall live for ever, emboss'd or graven
On the chalcedon gates and the streets pearl-paven :
The Thoughts of the just, at a flash transferr'd
From the wastes of earth to the courts of the Word,
The hopes abortive, the frustrate schemes,
  Shall lack not a place in the wond'rous session ;
The prayers of the Saints, their griefs, their dreams,
  Shall be manifest there in vision ;
For they live in the Mind Divine, their mould,
  That Mind Divine the unclouded mirror
Wherein the glorified Spirits behold
  All worlds, undimm'd by error.

VII.

Fling fire on the earth, O God,
  Consuming all things base!
Fling fire upon man, his soul and his blood,
  The fire of Thy Love and Grace:
That his heart once more to its natal place
Like a bondsman freed may rise,
Ascending for ever before Thy face
  From the altar of Sacrifice!

And thou, Love's comrade, Hope,
That giv'st to Wisdom strength, to Virtue scope,
That giv'st to man and nation
The on-rushing plumes of spiritual aspiration,
Van-courier of the ages, Faith's strong guide,
That still the attain'd foregoest for the descried:—
On, Seraph, on, through night and tempest winging!
  On heavenward, on, across the void, vast hollow!
And be it ours, to thy wide skirts close clinging
  Blindly, like babes, thy conquering flight to follow.
What though the storm of Time roar on beside us?
Though this world mock or chide us?
We shall not faint or fail until at last
The eternal shore is reach'd, all danger past!

May, 1859.

GLAUCÈ.

I LOVE you, pretty maid, for you are young:
I love you, pretty maid, for you are fair:
I love you, pretty maid, for you love me.

They tell me that, a babe, smiling you gazed
Upon the stars, with open, asking eyes,
And tremulous lips apart. Erelong, self-taught,
You found for every star and every flower
Legends and names and fables sweet and new.

O that when far away I still might see thee!
How oft, when wearied with the din of life
On thee my eyes would rest, thy Grecian heavens
Brightening that orbèd brow!—
Hesper should shine upon thee—lamp of Love,
Beneath whose radiance thou wert born. O Hesper!
Thee will I love and reverence evermore!

Bind up that shining hair into a knot
And let me see that polished neck of thine
Uprising from the bed snow-soft, snow-white
In which it rests so gracefully! What God
Hath drawn upon thy forehead's ivory plane
Those two clear streaks of sweet and glistening black
Lifted in earnest mirth or lovely awe?
Open those Pleiad eyes, liquid and tender,

And let me lose myself among their depths!
Caress me with thine infant hands, and tell me
Old tales divine that love makes ever new
Of Gods and men entoiled in flowery nets,
Of heroes sighing all their youth away,
And Troy, death-sentenced by those Argive eyes.

Come forth, dear maid, the day is calm and cool,
And bright though sunless. Like a long green scarf,
The tall Pines crowning yon grey promontory
In distant ether hang, and cut the sea.
But lovers better love the dell, for there
Each is the other's world.—How indolently
The tops of those pale poplars bend and sway
Over the violet-braided river-brim!
Whence comes their motion, for no wind is heard,
And the long grasses move not, nor the reeds?
Here we will sit, and watch the rushes lying
Like locks, along the leaden-colored stream
Far off—and thou, O child, shalt talk to me
Of Naiads and their loves. A blissful life
They lead who live beneath the flowing waters.
They cherish calm, and think the sea-weeds fair:
They love each other's beauty; love to stand
Among the lilies, holding back their tresses
And listening, with their gentle cheek reclined
Upon the flood, to some far melody
Of Pan or shepherd piping in lone woods
Until the unconscious tears run down their face.
Mild are their loves, nor burdensome their thoughts—
And would that such a life were mine and thine!

IONÈ.

IONE, fifteen years have o'er you passed,
And, taking nothing from you in their flight,
Have given you much. You look like one for whom
The day has morning only, time but Spring.
Your eyes are large and calm, your lips serene,
As if no Winter with your dreams commingled,
You that dream always, or that never dream!

Dear maid, you should have been a shepherdess—
But no: ill-tended then your flocks had strayed.
Young fawns you should have led; such fawns as once
The quivered Queen had spared to startle! Then
Within your hand a willow wand, your brow
Wreathed with red roses dabbled in warm rains,
How sweetly, with half-serious countenance,
Through the green alleys had you ta'en your way!
And they, your spotted train, how happily
Would they have gambolled by you—happiest she
The milk-white creature in the silver chain!

Ionè, lay the tapestry down: come forth—
No golden ringlet shall you add this morn
To bright Apollo: and poor Daphne there!
Without her verdant branches she must rest
Another day—a cruel tale, sweet girl!

You will not! Then farewell our loves for ever!
We are too far unlike: not Cyclops more

Unlike that Galatea whom he courted.
I love the loud-resounding sea divine;
I love the wintry sunset, and the stress
Inexorable of wide-wasting storms;
I love the waste of foam-washed promontories;
Thunder, and all portentous change that makes
The mind of mortals like to suns eclipsed
Waning in icy terrors. These to you
Are nothing. On the ivied banks you lie
In deep green valleys grey with noontide dew.
There bathe your feet in bubbling springs, your hands
Playing with the moist pansies near your face.

These bowers are musical with nightingales
Morning and noon and night. Among these rocks
A lovely life is that you lead; but I
Will make it lovelier with some pretty gift
If you are constant to me! Constant never
Was Nymph or Nereid: — like the waves they
change;—
O Nymph so change not thou! A boat I'll make
Scooped from a pine: yourself shall learn to row it;
Swifter than winds or sounds can fleet; or else
Your scarf shall be the sail, and you shall glide,
While the stars drop their light upon the bay,
On like a bird between the double heaven!
Are these but trivial joys? Ah me! fresh leaves
Gladden the forests; but no second life
Invests our branches—feathers new make bright

The birds; but when our affluent locks desert us,
No Spring restores them. Dried-up streams once
 more
The laughing Nymphs replenish; but man's life,
By fate drawn down and smothered in the sands,
Never looks up. Alas, my sweet Ionè,
Alcæus also loved; but in his arms
Finds rest no more the song-full Lesbian maid:
The indignant hand attesting Gods and men
Achilles lifts no more: to dust is turned
His harp that glittered through the wild sea spray,
Though the black wave falls yet on Ilion's shore.
All things must die—the Songs themselves, except
The devout hymn of grateful love; or hers,
The wild swan's, chaunting her death melody.

LYCIUS.

Lycius! the female race is all the same!
All variable, as the Poets tell us;
Mad through caprice — half way 'twixt men and
 children.

Acasta, mildest lake of all our maids,
Colder and calmer than a sacred well,
Is now more changed than Spring has changed these
 thickets:
Hers is the fault, not mine. Yourself shall judge.

From Epidaurus, where from three long days
With Nicias I had stayed, honoring the God,
If strength might thus mine aged Sire renerve,
Last evening we returned. The way was dull
And vexed with mountains: tired ere long was I
From warding off the oleander boughs
Which, as my comrade o'er the stream's dry bed
Pushed on, closed backward on my mule and me.
The flies maintained a melody unblest;
While Nicias, of his wreath Nemean proud,
Sang of the Satyrs and the Nymphs all day
Like one by Esculapius fever-smitten.
Arrived at eve, we bathed; and drank, and ate
Of figs and olives till our souls exulted.
Lastly we slept like gods. When morning shone,
So filled was I with weariness and sleep
That as a log till noon I lay; then rose,
And in the bath-room sat. While there I languished
Reading that old, divine and holy tale
Of sad Ismenè and Antigonè,
Two warm soft hands flung suddenly around me
Closed both my eyes; and a clear, shrill, sweet laughter
Told me that she it was, Acasta's self,
That brake upon my dreams. "What would you child?"
"Child, child," Acasta cried! "I am no child—
You do me wrong in calling me a child!
Come with me to the willowy river's brim:
There read, if you must read."

Her eyes not less
Than hands uplifted me, and forth we strayed.
O'er all the Argolic plain Apollo's shafts
So fiercely fell, methought the least had slain
A second Python. From that theatre
Hewn in the rock the Argive tumult rolled!
Before the fane of Juno seven vast oxen
Lowed loud, denouncing Heaven ere yet they fell:
While from the hill-girt meadows rose a scent
So rich, the salt sea odors vainly strove
To pierce those fumes it curled about my brain,
And sting the nimbler spirits. Nodding I watched
The pale herbs from the parched bank that trailed
Bathing delighted in voluptuous cold,
And scarcely swayed by that slow winding stream.
I heard a sigh—I asked not whence it came.
At last a breeze went by, to glossy waves
Rippling the steely flood: I noted then
The reflex of the poplar stem thereon
Curled into spiral wreaths, and toward me darting
Like a long, shining water-snake: I laughed
To see its restlessness. Acasta cried,
"Read—if you will not speak—or look at me!"
Unconsciously I glanced upon the page,
Bent o'er it, and began to chaunt that chorus,
"Favored by Love are they that love not deeply,"
When, leaping from my side, she snatched the book,
Into the river dashed it, bounded by,
And, no word spoken, left me there alone.

Lycius! I see you smile; but know you not
Nothing is trifling which the Muse records,
And lovers love to muse on? Let the Gods
Act as to them seems fitting. Hermes loved—
Phœbus loved also—but the hearts of Gods
Are everlasting like the suns and stars,
Their loves as transient as the clouds. For me
A peaceful life is all I seek, and far
Removed from cares and all the female kind!

LINES WRITTEN UNDER DELPHI.

I.

My goal is reached—homeward henceforth my way.
I have beheld Earth's glories. Had the eyes
Of those I love reposed on them with mine,
No future wish to roam beyond the range
Of one green pasture circling one clear lake
Itself by one soft woodland girt around,
Could touch this heart. My pilgrimage is made.

II.

I have seen Delphi: I no more shall see it.
I go contented, having seen it once;
Yet here awhile remain, prisoner well-pleased
Of reboant winds. Within this mountain cove

Their sound alone finds entrance. Lightly the waves
(Rolled from the outer to the inner bay)
Dance in blue silver o'er the silver sands ;
While, like a chain-bound antelope by some child
Mocked oft with tempting hand and fruit upholden,
Our quick caique vaults up among the reeds,
The ripples that plunge past it upward sending
O'er the grey margin matted with sea-pink
Ripplings of light. The moon is veiled ; a mile
Below the mountain's eastern range it hangs :
Yon gleam is but its reflex, from white clouds
Scattered along Parnassian peaks of snow.

III.

I see but waves and snows. Memory alone
Fruition hath of what this morn was mine :
O'er many a beauteous scene at once she broods,
And feeds on joys without confusion blent
Like mingling sounds or odors. Now she rests
On that serene expanse (the confluence
Of three long vales) in sweetness upward heaved,
Ample and rich as Juno's breast what time
The Thunderer's breath in sleep moves over it :
Bathes in those runnels now, that raced together
This morn as at some festival of streams,
Through arbutus and ilex, wafting each
Upon its glassy track a several breeze,
Each with its tale of joy or playful sadness.
Fair nymphs, by great Apollo's fall untouched !
Sing, sing, for ever ! When did golden Phœbus
Look sad one moment for a fair nymph's fall ?

IV.

A still, black glen—below, a stream-like copse
Of hoary olives ; rocks like walls beside,
Never by Centaur trod, though these fresh gales
Give man the Centaur's strength ! Again I mount,
From cliff to cliff, from height to height ascending ;
Glitters Castalia's Fount ; I see, I touch it !
That Rift once more I reach, the Oracular seat,
Whose arching rocks half meet in air suspense ;
'Twixt them is one blue streak of heaven ; hard by
Dim Temples hollowed in the stone, for rites
Mysterious shaped, or mansions of the dead :
Released, I turn, and see, far, far below,
A vale so rich in floral garniture,
And odors from the orange and the sea,
So girt with white peaks flashing from sky chasms,
So lighted with the vast blue dome of Heaven,
So lulled with music from the winds and waves,
The guest of Phœbus claps his hands and shouts,
"There is but one such spot ; from Heaven Apollo
Beheld ;—and chose it for his earthly shrine !"

V.

Phœbus Apollo ! loftiest shape of all
That glorified the range of Grecian song,
By Poet hymned or Shepherd when the rocks
Confessed the first bright impress of thy feet ;
By many an old man praised when Thracian blasts
Sang loud, and pine-wood stores began to fail ;

Served by the sick man searching hill and plain
For herb assuasive ; courted by sad maids
On whose pure lips thy fancied kiss descended
Softly as vernal beam on primrose cold :
By Fortune's troubled Favorites ofttime sued
For dubious answer, then when Fate malign,
Beyond the horizon of high Hopes ascending,
Her long fell glance had cast on them—Apollo
Who, what wert thou ? Let those who read thy tale
In clouded chambers of the North, reply,
"An empty dream !" —bid them fling far the scroll,
The dusty parchment fling aside for ever,
Or scan with light from thy Parnassian skies !
For Commentator's lamp give them thine orb
Flaming on high, transfixing cloud and wave
Or noon-tide laurel—(as the Zephyr strikes,
Daphne once more shrinks trembling from thy beams)—
Were these but fancies ? O'er the world they reared
The only empire verily universal
Founded by man—for Fancy heralds Thought ;
Thought Act ; and nations Are as they Believe.
Strong were such fancies,—strong not less than fair !
The plant spontaneous of Society
In Greece, by them with stellar power was dewed,
And, nursed by their far influence, grew and flourished :
A state of order and fair fellowship,
Man with man walking, not in barbarous sort
His own prey finding, each, and his own God ;
A state of freedom, not by outward force

Compressed, or ice-like knit by negatives ;
A frank communion of deep thoughts with glad,
Light cares with grave—a changeful melody
Varying each moment, yet in soul the same ;
A temple raised for beauty and defence ·
An armed dance held for a festival ;
A balanced scheme that gave each power a limit,
Each toil a crown, and every art her Muse !
O frank and graceful life of Grecian years !
Whence came thy model ? From the Grecian heaven
The loves and wars of Gods, their works and ways,
Their several spheres distinct yet interwreathed,
By Greece were copied on a lesser stage.
Our thoughts soar high to light our paths on earth.
Terrestrial circles from celestial take
Their impress in man's science. Stars unreached
Our course o'er ocean guide. Orphean sounds
The walls of cities raised ;—thus mythic bards
For all the legislators legislated !

VI.

Yet these were idols : such as worshipped these
Were worshippers of idols. Holy and True !
How many are there not idolaters ?
Traditions, Systems, Passion, Interest, Power—
Are these not idols ? Ay, the worst of idols !
Not that men worship these ; but that before them
Down-bent, the faculty that worship pays
Shrivels and dies. Man's spirit alone adores,
And can adore but Spirit. What is not God,
Howe'er our fears may crouch, or habit grovel,

Or sensuous fancy dote, we worship not :
Unless God look on man, he cannot pray ;
Such is Idolatry's masked Atheism !
—Yes, these were idols, for man made them idols.
By a corrupt heart all things are corrupted,
God's works alike or products of the mind.
The Soul, insurgent 'gainst its Maker, lacks
The strength its vassal powers to rule. The Will
To blind Caprice grows subject : Reason, torn
From Faith, becomes the Understanding's slave ;
And Passion's self in Appetite is lost.
Then Idols dominate—Despots by Self-will
Set up, where Law and Faith alike are dead,
To awe the anarchy of godless souls.
Nought but a Worship, spiritual and pure,
Profound, habitual, strong through loving awe,
A true heart's tribute to the God of Truth ;
From selfishness redeemed, and so from sense
Secured, though conversant with shapes of sense,
Nought but such Worship, with spontaneous force
From our whole Being equably ascending
As odor from a flower or fount's clear breath,
Redeems us from Idolatry. In vain
Are proudly wise appeals that deprecate
Rites superstitious ; vain are words though shrill
With scorn—stark, pointed finger,—forehead ridged
With blear-eyed Scepticism's myriad wrinkles :
Saintly we must be, or Idolatrous.
After his image Man creates him Gods,
Kneading the symbol (as a symbol holy
And salutary) to a form compact

With servile soul and mean mechanic hand—
Thus to their native dust his Thoughts return,
Abashed, and of mortality convinced.

VII.

At Salem was the Law. The Holy Land
Its orient terrace by the ocean reared,
And thereon walked the Holy One, at cool
Of the world's morn : there visible state He kept.
At Salem was the Law on stone inscribed ;
But over all the world, within man's heart
The unwritten Law abode, from earliest time
Upon our nature stampt, nor wholly lost.
Men saw it, loved it, praised—and disobeyed.
Therefore the Conscience, whose applausive voice
Their march triumphant should have led with joy
To all perfection, from a desert pealed
The Baptist's note alone—" Repent, repent ;"
And men with song more flattering filled their ears.
Yet still the undersong was holy ! long
(Though cast on days unblest, though sin-defiled)
The mind accepted, yea the heart revered,
That which the Will lacked strength to follow. Conscience
(Her crown monarchal first, her fillet next
Snatched from her sacred brows) a minstrel's wreath
Assumed ; and breathed in song her soul abroad :

On outcast Duty's grave she, with her tears
Dropt flowers funereal of surpassing beauty ;
With Reason walked ; the right path indicated,
Though her imperative voice was heard no more.
Nor spake in vain. Man, fallen man was great,
Remembering ancient greatness : Hymn and tale
Held, each, some portion of dismembered Truth,
Severely sung by Poets wise and brave.
They sang of Justice, God's great attribute,
With tragic buskin, and a larger stride
Following the fated victim step by step.
They sang of Love crowning the toils of life :
Of Joy they sang ; for Joy, that gift divine,
Primal and wingèd creature, with full breath
Through all the elastic limbs of Grecian fable
Poured her redundant life ; the noble tongue
Strong as the brazen clang of ringing arms,
With resonance of liquid sounds enriching
Sweet as the music-laughter of the Gods :—
Of heavenly Pity, Prophet-like they sang ;
And, feeling after Good though finding not,
Of Him, that Good not yet in Flesh revealed,
By ceaseless vigils, tears, and lifted palms,
And yearnings infinite and unrepressed,
A separate and authentic witness bore.
Thus was the end foreshown. Thus Error's "cloud
Turned forth its silver lining on the night."
Thus too—for us at least a precious gift,
Dear for the lore it grasped, by all it lacked
Made strong not less vain-glorious thoughts to chide,
Wisdom shone forth—but not for men unwise :

Her beams but taint the dead. Man's Guilt and Woe
She proved—and her own Helplessness confessed.
Such were her two great functions. Woe to those
Who live with Art for Faith, and Bards for Priests!
These are supplanted: Sense their loftiest hopes
Will sap; and Fiends usurp their oracles!

VIII.

Olympian dreams, farewell! your spell is past:
I turn from you away! From Eros' self,
From heavenly Beauty on thy crystal brow
Uranian Venus, starred in gentlest light,
From thee, Prometheus, chained on Caucasus,
Iȯ from thee, sad wanderer o'er the earth,
From thee great Hercules, the son of Heaven
And of Humanity held long in pain;
Heroic among men; by labors tried;
Descending to the Shades, and leading thence
The Lost; while infant still a Serpent-slayer;
In death a dread and mystic Sacrifice—
From thee, more high than all, from thee, Apollo!
Light of the world whose sacred beam, like words,
Illustrated the forehead of the earth;
Supreme of Harmonists, whose song flowed forth
Pure from that light; great slayer of the Serpent
That mocked thy Mother; master of that art
Healing man's ancient wound; Oracular:
Secretly speaking wisdom to the just;

Openly to the lost from lips unheeded
Like thy Cassandra's flinging it to waste—
Phœbus Apollo! here at thy chief shrine
From thee I turn; and stern confession make
That not the vilest weed yon ripple casts
Here at my feet, but holds a loftier gift
Than all the Grecian Legends. Let them go—
Because the mind of man they lifted up,
But corruptible instincts left to grovel
On Nature's common plane—year and below it;
Because they slightly healed the People's wound:
And sought in genial fancy, finite hopes,
Proportioned life, and dialectic Art,
A substitute for Virtue; and because
They gave for nothing that which Faith should earn,
Casting the pearls of Truth 'neath bestial feet:—
Because they washed the outside of the cup,
And dropped a thin veil o'er the face of Death;
Because they neither brought man to his God,
Nor let him feel his weakness—let them go!
Wisdom that raises not her sons is Folly:
Truth in its unity alone is Truth.

IX.

What now is Delphi? Where that temple now
Dreadful to kings; with votive offerings stored,
Tripod, or golden throne from furthest lands,
Or ingot huge? Where now that tremulous stone,
Centre of all things deemed—Earth's beating heart?

What now is Delphi ? yea, or Hellas' self,
With all her various States ; epitome
Of Nations ; stage whereon in little space
Forecasting Time rehearsed his thousand parts ?
Sparta's one camp—the sacred plain of Thebes ;
That plain, pious as rich, whence grateful Ceres
The hand that blesses Earth upraised to Heaven—
The unboastful freedom of Arcadian vales—
Athens with Academic Arts, and ships
Far-seen from pillared headlands ? Where, O where
Olympia's chariot-course that bent the eyes
Of Greece on one small ring shining like fire—
Or they, that sacred Council, at whose nod
King and Republic trembled ? Gone for ever !
Vine on the wave diffused, budding with Isles ;
Bower of young Earth, wherein the East and West,
Wedded, their beauteous progeny upreared ;
Hellas, by Nature blest, by Freedom nursed,
By Providence led on through discipline
Of change, till that Philosophy was formed
Which made one City man's perpetual Teacher—
Hellas is past ! A lamentable voice
Forth from the caverns of Antiquity
Issuing in mystery, answers, Where is Egypt ?
Egypt of magic craft and starry lore,
Eternal brooder on the unknown Past
Through the long vista of her Kings and Priests
Descried, as setting Moon beyond the length
Of forest aisle, or desert colonnade ;
Eldest of nations, and apart, like Night
Dark-veiled amid the synod of the Gods ?

The sun and stars with gaze alternate wonder
At pyramids sand-drowned, and long processions
Now petrified to lines of marble shapes
That lead to Sphinx-girt Cities of the Dead !
Where now is Babylon, mighty by peace
And gold, and men countless as forest leaves ?
Persia, the Macedonian, Carthage, Tyre ?
All gone—restored to earth ! Great Rome herself,
Haughty with arcs of triumph, theatres
Sphered to embrace all Nations and their Gods ;
Roads from one centre piercing lands remote ;
Bridges, fit type of Conquest's giant stride ;
Great Rome herself, empire of War and Law—
Yoking far regions—harrowing those fields
Reserved for Christian seed—Great Rome herself
Was, and is not ! The eternal edict stands :
The power from God which comes not, drops and
dies.

X.

Hark, to that sound ! yon ocean Eagle drives
The mist of morn before her, seaward launched
From her loved nest on Delphi. She, though stern,
Can love—a divine instinct, that outlasts
Phœbus, thy fabulous honors ! Far away
The storms are dying, and the night-bird pours,
Encouraged thus, her swift and rapturous song.
Ah ! when that song is over, I depart !

Return, my wandering thoughts ! the ascended Moon
Smiles on her Brother's peaks, and many a ridge
Her glance solicits ; many a stirring wood
Exults in her strong radiance as she glides
On from the pine gulf to the gulf of clouds.
Return, my thoughts ! the innumerous cedar cones
Of Lebanon must lull you now no longer ;
Nor fall of Empires with as soft a sound.
O'er famed Colonos stoop no more in trance,
Eyeing the city towers. No longer muse,
With mind divided, though a single heart,
On legend—true or erring ! Earth can yield
No scene more fair than this—and Nature's beauty
Is ever irreproachable. Return !
A long breath take of this ambrosial clime
Ere lost the sweetness : sigh, yet be content :
Fill here your golden urns ; be fresh for ever !

XI.

I have beheld Mont Blanc ; in eminence,
Though seated, over all his standing sons,
Unearthly Eremite whose cell is Heaven ;
His glacier beard forth-streaming to his feet
Beyond his cloudy raiment. I have gazed
On Rome ; have watched it from the Alban hill ;
Have marked that dome supreme, its mitred crown,
Dilate at sunset o'er the Latian bounds.
Byzantium I have seen ; first capital

That owned the Faith; whose rising up once more
Shall be as mighty gates their 'heads uplifting'
O'er all the earth, 'for God to enter in.'
These three have I beheld: to these henceforth
I add a fourth to stand with these for ever.
On rock or tree my name I dare not trace—
Delphi! stamp thou thine image on my heart.

THE DIGNITY OF SORROW.

I.

I HAVE not seen you since the Shadow fell
  From Heaven against your door:
I know not if you bear your Sorrow well:
I only know your hearth is cold; your floor
Will hear that soft and gliding tread no more.

II.

I know our ancient friendship now is over:
  I can love still, and so will not complain:
    I have not loved in vain;
Taught long that Art of Sadness to discover
    Which draws stern solace from the wells of Pain.
You love the Dead alone; or you have lost
The power and life of Love in Time's untimely frost.

III.

You have stood up in the great Monarch's court—
The court of Death: in spirit you have seen
His lonely shades serene
Where all the mighty men of old resort.
The eyes of Proserpine,
Heavy and black, have rested upon thine.
Her vintage, wine from laurel-berries prest,
You raised—and laid you then the dark urn down,
Scared by that Queen's inevitable frown,
Just as the marble touched your panting breast?
Oh! in the mirror of that poison cold
What Shadow or what Shape did you behold?

IV.

And she is dead: and you have long been dying:
And are recovered, and live on! O Friend!
Say, what shall be the end
Of leaf-lamenting boughs and wintry sighing?
When will the woods that moan
Resume their green array?
When will the dull, sad clouds be overblown,
And a calm sunset close our stormy day?

V.

My thoughts pursue you still. I call them back.
Once more they seek you, like the birds that rise
Up from their reeds, and in a winding track
Circle the field wherein their forage lies;—
Or like some poor and downcast Pensioner,
Depressed and timid, though his head be grey,

That moves with curving steps to greet his
Lord,
Whom he hath watched all day—
Yet lets him pass away without a word;
And gazes on his footsteps from afar.

SONG.

I.

A BRIGHTENED Sorrow veils her face,
Sweet thoughts with thoughts forlorn,
And playful sadness, like the grace
Of some autumnal morn;
When birds new-waked, like sprightly elves,
The languid echoes rouse,
And infant Zephyrs make themselves
Familiar with old boughs.

II.

All round our hearts the Maiden's hair
Its own soft shade doth fling:
Her sigh perfumes the forest air,
Like eve—but eve in Spring!
When Spring precipitates her flow;
And Summer, swift to greet her,
Breathes, every night, a warmer glow
Half through the dusk to meet her.

A WANDERER'S MUSINGS AT ROME.

THANKS be to Heaven! yon grove of sombre pines,
Whose several tops, like feathers in one wing
Folded o'er one another, hang in air,
From the great City hides me! From its sound,
Low but mysterious, urgent, agitating,
Not distance only, but those rifted walls
Immense (how oft at noontide have I watched
The long green lizard from their fissures glance,
And glide from thicket-mantled tower to tower)
Not less protect me. Thanks once more to Heaven!
This nook in which I lie, this grassy isle
Amid the burnt brake nested, hath no name:
No legend haunts it. Unalarmed I turn,
Confronted by no despot from the grave,
By no inscription challenged. If this spot
Was trod of old by consul or by King,
It is my privilege to be ignorant:
They lived and died. If here the Roman Twins
Tugged at the she-wolf, they have had their day:
Yon lambs have now their hour; and I, a stranger,
Following the path their feet have worn, here find
Their cool recess, and share it. Pretty thrush!
Possess thy soul in peace, and sing at will,
Sharpening thy clear expostulating note,
Or softening, 'mid the branches. Murmuring stream!
Sufficient to solicit and reward
An unconstrained attention, thou to me
(A lover of the torrents ere I heard them)
This day art dearer far than Alpine floods

In whose abysmal voices all the sounds
Of all the vales are met and reconciled.
From admiration I desire repose;
Rest from that household foe, a beating heart;
Yea, from all thought exemption, save such thoughts
As, lightly wafted toward us, leave us lightly,
And, like the salutation of those winds
That curl yon ilex leaves, if sweets they bring,
Bequeath a sweeter freshness. Three weeks since
To me this dell of grass had seemed a prison,
And hours here spent ignoblest apathy.
The change! whence comes it? Fevered nights and
days
Make answer! Answer thou, mysterious City,
Whose shade eclipsed the world a thousand years!
Tomb, aqueduct, and porch I visited,
And strove with adulating thoughts to clasp;
And could not: for as some vast tree, the sire
Of woods, flings off the span of infant arms,
So by its breadth and compass Rome rebuked
My sympathies. The "lesser," verily,
"Is of the greater blessed;" and Love, a gift,
Falls back, repulsed, from that which scorns its aid;
From that which, solitary in its vastness,
Admits no measurement, nor condescends
To be in portions grasped; from that which yields
No crevice to the climber's hand or foot;
Whose height o'erawes our winged aspirations,
Like some steep cliff of ocean in whose shade
The circling sea-birds wail. And yet, unable
With soul-unburdening love to clasp thee, Rome,
Much more was I unable to forget thee.

I mused in city wastes, where pitying Earth
Takes back into her breast huge fragments strewn
Around, like bones of savage beasts extinct:
From wreck to wreck I roamed: my very dreams
Nested in obscure haunts and vaults unhealthy:
Ruin on ruin pressed, rivals in death,
Like grave dislodging grave in churchyard choked:
Triumphant Pillar, and vainglorious Arch
Towered in blue sky: voluptuous Baths laid bare
Colossal vice: and one great* Temple meet
For that promiscuous worship Statecraft loves,
Lifted its haughty dome and pillared front.
I sought Cornelia's house, but found instead
The Cæsars' Palace, and the Coliseum,
That theatre of blood, where sat enthroned,
Swollen with the rage of Roman merriment,
The Roman People—Earth's chief idol served
With human victims!

From its own excess
Triumphant Evil suffers confutation:
Not here where, tested by the extreme it reached,
The Imperial instinct stands unmasked—not here
Can the sword's conquests subjugate the soul.
A lucid interval perforce is ours,
By these memorials quelled. The race that here
Trod down their brethren daily, in their day
Might plead some poor excuse. Each war to them
Some singular necessity might urge,
Or final peace impledge: but we who stand

* The Pantheon.

Outfaced by all the congregated trophies
They reared that gloried in their shame ; who pace
O'er Tullia's way to reach Domitian's halls ;
Who in one choir behold the British Queen
And earliest Sabine maid ; who hear at once
The wail of Veii and the falling roofs
Of Carthage, till monotonous becomes
The cry of nations, and the tale of blood
A tedious iteration ; we who scan,
Marbled in Rome, the form of injured Earth,
And trace her wounds, and count each accurate scar
In that dread victim by Rome's talon and beak
Grav'n and recorded—we are scantly moved
On martial sway to dote. What magic, then,
Draws us to Rome ? What Spirit bids the nations
Send up their tribes to one Metropolis—
To her whom many hate—whom many fear—
Where lies the spell ? Luxurious wealth has spread
No velvet o'er the Roman streets, nor hung
The spoils of Cashmeer, Persia, Samarcand,
On either side the way. No flattering dream
Of Fame restored, and ancient life renewed,
Looks forth from heaven into a young man's eyes,
Then drops, and plants its tent on Tyber's bank.
The tawny Tyber is no mountain rill
Where Fancy slakes her thirst. The sage shrinks back,
And in the Roman Sibyl's bleeding book
Will read no line—
The future here is mortgaged to the past ;
Hope breathes no temporal promise o'er that plain
On which malaria broods : amid the tombs

Her foot moves slowly; and where Hope is lame
The social forces languish.

Whence the spell
That draws us, then, to Rome? In arms, no more
It lives. Abides it ambushed then in Art?
The reign of Art is over. To uprear
A prostrate column on its crumbling base
Is here her chief of triumphs! Art is dead!
Here as in every land. In death gold-robed
Her soul-less body, stretched across the street,
Blocks up the public ways. The artist's study,
Of old a hermit's cell, where Mind recluse,
Pillowed on stores aforetime wrung from Thought
By Passion, by Experience drawn from Life,
Saw visions as in Patmos, and set forth
The shapes it saw, is now a wrangling shop
In all the regal cities of the world,
For them that buy and sell. In ancient time
The painter was a preacher, whose sage hand
Pictured high thought. If Martyrdom that thought,
The radiant face of confessor unmoved
Expressed full well that death which is a birth
Into the realms of light. If Faith that thought,
Lo! where St. Jerome, eremite and saint,
A dweller among rocks, himself a rock,
Wasted and gaunt, fast-worn, and vigil-blind,
Dying, draws near in faith (with both hands clasped,
And awe-struck lip) to Him the invisible,
And on that "Last Communion" hanging, rests
The weight of all his being! If he mused
On Purity, ah! mark that seer (nor young,

Nor female) who a lily holds and reads
Writ in its depths the life white-robed of them
Who follow still the Lamb ! Art, Art of old,
Handmaid of Faith—prophet that witness bore
Of God, not self, nor came in her own name ;
Initiate in the Ideal Truth that spans
The actual scope of things, and thence advanced
To stand great Nature's meek Interpreter ;
Is now a painted Queen, and keeps her court
In palace halls whose marble labyrinths
Like cities peopled by a race of stone,
Branch forth unnumbered. Breathlessly we turn ;
And sigh for stillness, sigh for utter peace,
For darkness, or assuasive twilight drawn
In dewy gentleness o'er pastures broad
Whose cool serenity of blue and green
Lures the tense spirit forth, and in a bath
Of relaxation soft soothes and contents it—
Too much of ostentatious aid unasked !
Are we so weak within ? Can we advance
No step without a crutch ? no lessons learn,
Save lessons thrust upon us ? Can we catch
In Nature's music manifold no voice
But sad confessions of her nothingness ?
Trust we in dead things only ? Nature lives !
Her moving clouds, the rapture of her waves,
Her rural haunts domestic—nooks sun-warmed,
Endeared to babe and greybeard—her expanse
Of fruitful plains, with hamlet, hall, and tower,
Homestead and hedge, in autumn's glistening air
Drawn out at eve, or by the ferment dazed
Of summer sunrise, or on vernal noon

Melting in pearly distance like our dreams
For man's far welfare ; her mysterious glens,
That with the substance of one shade are thronged,
And other habitant have none, that speak
Of God and God alone, transfix the heart
With wisdom less imposed on man than won
From man's resources. Nature's demonstrations,
Maternal, not scholastic, need have none
Of diagram. Her own face is their proof,
Subduing in the pathos of its smiles,
Or power of eye : and being infinite,
Her life is all in every part ; her lore
In lowliest shape is perfect. Thou, frail flower,
Anemone ! that near my grassy couch,
By a breath shaken which I scarcely feel,
Thy gracious head as though in worship bowest
Down on thy mother's lap—in thee, in thee
(I seek no further) lives that Power supreme,
Whereof the artists boast. Immaculate Beauty
In thy humility doth dominate,
Is of thy tremblings proud, and, gladly clothed
In thy thin garb of colors and fair forms,
Looks up and smiles. I pluck thee from thy bed—
Lie lightly on a breast that weary grows
Of haughtier burdens ! Cool a fevered heart,
That seeking better things hath sought in vain !
Be thou my monitor : let me sum up.
What have I chiefly learned from human life ?
That life as brief as thine is to be praised :
That life's best blessings are the joys we tread
To death unseen, chasing inventions vain :
That He who made thee, made the heavens and earth,

And man; and that in Him is life alone;
To serve Him freedom and to know Him peace.—
Thine ancestress that bloomed in Paradise,
Possessed no softer voice to celebrate
(Joining the visual chorus of all worlds)
Her great Creator's glory!

Hark that peal!
From countless domes that high in sunlight shake,
A thousand bells roll forth their harmonies:
The City, by the noontide flame oppressed,
And sheltered long in sleep, awakes. Even now,
Along the Pincian steep, with youthful step
To dignity subdued, collegiate trains
Precede their grave preceptors. Courts grass-grown,
That echoed long some fountain's lonely splash,
Now ring more loudly, by the red wheels dinned
Of prince, or prelate of the Church intent
On some majestic Rite. That peal again!
And now the linked Procession moves abroad,
Untwining slowly its voluminous folds:
It pauses—through the dusky archway drawn,
It vanishes—upcoiled at last, and still,
Girdling the Coliseum's central Cross,
The sacred pageant rests. With stealthy motion
So slid the Esculapian snake of old
Forth from the darkness. In Hesperian isle
So rested, coiled around the mystic stem,
The watcher of the fruit. The day draws on:
The multitudinous thrill of quickening life
Vibrates through all the city, while its blood
Flows back from vein to vein. That sound prevails

In convent walks by rustling robe trailed o'er;
Like hum of insects unbeheld it throbs
Through orange-scented, cloistral gardens dim;
It deepens with the concourse onward borne
Between those statued saints that guard thy bridge,
St. Angelo, and past the Adrian Tomb
Where at the Church's foot an Empire sleeps;
It swells within those Colonnades whose arms
Receive once more the concourse from all lands—
The lofty English noble, student pale
From Germany, diplomatist from France,
Far Grecian patriarch, or Armenian priest,
Or Royal Exile. From thy marble roofs,
St. Peter's, in whose fastnesses abide,
Like Arab tribe encamped, the bands ordained
To guard them from the aggressive elements—
From those aërial roofs to whispering depths
Of crypts where kneels the cowled monk alone,
The murmur spreads like one broad wind that lifts,
Ere morn the sighing shrouds of fleet becalmed:
The churches fill; the relics forth are brought:
Screened by rich fretwork the monastic apse
Resounds the hoarse chant, like an ocean cave:
And long ere yet those obelisks which once
Shadowed the Nile, o'er courts Basilican
Project their evening shades, like silver stars
Before white altars glimmering lights shall burn,
And solitary suppliants lift their hands
To Christ, for ever Present, to His Saints,
And to His Martyrs, whom the Catacombs
Hid in their sunless bosoms.

Rome, O Rome!
Surely thy Strength is here! Three hundred years
The faithful people lived among the Tombs;
The Catacombs were their Metropolis.
There in the darkness thirty Pontiffs ruled;
There won the crown of martyrdom. The Rite,
Dread, and tremendous, yoking earth and heaven,
The Christian Sacrifice, was offered there,
A tomb the altar, and, for relics, blood
Of him who last confessed. The pictured walls
To Mary and to Peter witness still.
Here is thy Strength, O Rome! Sun-clad, above,
The Emperor triumphed, and the People triumphed!
The Nubian lion, and the Lybian pard
Roared for their prey! Above thy tawny wave,
Tyber, the world's increase went up each day:
Daily from Rome the Legions passed whose arms
Flashed back in turn the sunrise of all lands:
Through every gate the embassies of Kings
Advanced with gifts. But in the Catacombs
The Faithful People, circled by their dead,
Worshipped their God in peace. Three hundred years
Passed like three days: and lo! that Power went forth
Which conquered Death. Then Hell gave up her prey:
That hour the kingdoms of this world became
The kingdoms of the Lord, and of His Christ:
The Prince of this world, from his throne, upreared
On subject thrones of every land, was hurled:
The Pagan victories then their meaning found:
The Empire last and mightiest that absorbed
All its precursors, lay a ruin: God
His Family on earth a Kingdom made,

And Sion built on buried Babylon!
The Sacrament of Obedience paid to God
Through Man, His Vicar, glorified that hour,
Subjection; and the Apostles reigned at Rome—
Reigned from their tombs, and conquered from their
 dust!
Behold the mystery of the ages! Man
Wrought it unconscious! History is mad,
Or finds its meaning here. One mystery vast
Solves here Philosophy's uncounted riddles:
Time with its tumults here is harmonized:
Hope here is found or nowhere!

As a mist
That strives no longer, swept by quiring winds
From some peak'd mountain, my oppression leaves
 me!
Great Rome is mine at last! Refreshed I rise;
And gales of life from that celestial bourne
Whereto we tend strike on me. With soft shock
Yon almond bower lets fall its summer snow,
The sun is setting. The despotic day
Which, blessing earth with increase, suffered none
To lift a grateful eye, hath heard his doom;
And round him folds his robes, blood-stained and
 golden,
With dignity to die. Like haughty hopes
From one reduced by sickness, from the clouds
Their pageantries are melting: and ere long
No hue save that translucent, tender green,
Will speak of pomps gone by. The increasing wind,
Incumbent on the pine-grove's summit broad,

Gathers in volumed strength: within its vaults
An omnipresent and persistent whisper
Waxes in loudness. Well, might I believe
The hosts angelic, who with guardian care,
Urging belike the seasons in their course,
Circle the earth, even now on wings outspread
Were rustling o'er me, countless as sea-sands.
Glorious and blessed Armies! free ye are
From man's uncertainties, and free not less
From man's illusions! Passing in one flight
Calpë and Athens—all that makes renowned
This many-mountained, many-citied globe,
To you our schemes of worldly rule must seem
Like some poor maniac's towers in charcoal sketched
(Airy possession) on his cell's bare wall;
Our science like that knowledge won from touch
By one born blind; our arts like gems minute,
Poor fragments crumbled from your spheres eterne!
Pity us, then, bright Spirits, for ye know
The weakness of our strength; the poverty
Ye know, which we for wealth misdeem—exchanging
The gold of Truth Unchangeable and One
(Shared, not divided) for the baser coin
Of Truth in portions, scattered through the world.
Ye know the sad vacuity of hearts
With trifles filled, and thence from Him averse
In love for Whom is clasped the love of all things,
And their possession. Starlike in your ken,
By distance, and the barriers of the nations,
And all that haze which men call ancientness,
Unfooled ye are. For you the Church of God,
Unwrinkled as the ocean, wears for aye

Her Pentecostal glory. All things that live,
And die not—all Realities divine,
Live in the light of an eternal Present
And prime perpetual. Him whom we revere
As patriarch, ye behold a white-haired babe,
Poor, heaven-protected infant of fourscore:
His course accomplished, still in him ye note
His mother's new delight—a bud dried up;
Dropt from the human stem at noon; ere night
Blown forth into the darkness. Spirits blest!
The sun that runs before you rises ever;
For ever sets; reigns ever throned at noon:
Past, Present, Future mingle in your sight,
And Time its tortuous stream spreads to a lake
Girt by, and imaging, Eternity,
Between whose mirror and the infinite vault
Ye in the radiance bask!

Bask on, bright Spirits!
Bathe in the beam of Godhead; or fulfil
With awe your ministries of love, in Man
That seeing which they saw not who of old
The Galilean mocked. By death absolved—
By perfected Obedience rendered free,
Man o'er the ruins of the world shall rise;
Yea, from the height of heaven, the throne of God,
Shall gaze upon a universe renewed—
His Image o'er that universe shall cast
And o'er your shining hosts—his hand shall raise;
And, with the Voice Supreme blending his own,
Shall bless you, and pronounce you "very good."

SONG.

He found me sitting among flowers,
My Mother's, and my own;
Whiling away too happy hours
With songs of doleful tone.

My Sister came, and laid her book
Upon my lap: and He,
He too into the page would look,
And asked no leave of me.

The little frightened creature laid
Her face upon my knee—
"You teach your sister, pretty maid;
And I would fain teach thee."

He taught me Joy more blest, more brief
Than that mild vernal weather:
He taught me Love; he taught me Grief:
He taught me both together.

Give me a sun-warmed nook to cry in!
And a wall-flower's perfume—
A nook to cry in, and to die in,
'Mid the Ruin's gloom.

PERSECUTION.

I.

THERE was silence in the heavens
  When the Son of Man was led
From the Garden to the Judgment;
  Sudden silence, strange, and dread!
  All along the empyreal coasts,
  On their knees the immortal hosts
  Watched, with sad and wondering eyes,
  That tremendous sacrifice.

II.

There was silence in the heavens
  When the Priest his garment tore;
Silence when that Twain accursed
  Their false witness faintly bore.
  Silence (though a tremor crept
  O'er their ranks) the Angels kept
  While that judge, dismayed though proud,
  Wash'd his hands before the crowd.

III.

But when Christ His cross was bearing,
  Fainting oft, by slow degrees,
Then went forth the angelic thunder,
  Of legions rising from their knees.

Each bright Spirit grasped a brand;
And lightning flashed from band to band:
An instant more had launched them forth,
Avenging terrors, to the earth.

IV.

Then from God there fell a glory,
Round and o'er that multitude;
And by every fervent Angel
With hushing hand another stood—
Another, never seen before,
Stood one moment and no more!
—Peace, brethren, peace! to us is given
Suffering: vengeance is for Heaven!

LINES WRITTEN BESIDE THE LAGO VARESE.

(See Henry Taylor's Poem, entitled "Lago Varese.")

I.

STILL rise around that lake well sung
New growths as boon and good
As when, by sunshine saddened, long
Beside its margin stood
That northern youth, and o'er it breathed a lay
Which praised things beauteous, mourning their decay.

II.

As then great Nature, "kind to sloth,"
Lets drop o'er all the land
Her gifts, the fair and fruitful both,
Into the sleeper's hand:
On golden ground once more she paints as then
The cistus bower, and convent-brighten'd glen.

III.

Still o'er the flashing waters lean
The mulberry and the maize,
And roof of vines whose purple screen
Tempers those piercing rays,
Which here forego their fiercer shafts, and sleep,
Subdued, in crimson cells, and verdurous chambers deep.

IV.

And still in many a sandy creek
Light waves run on and up,
While the foam-bubbles winking break
Around their channell'd cup:
Against the rock they toss the bleeding gourd,
Or fret on marble stair and skiff unmoor'd.

V.

Fulfill'd thus far the Poet's words:—
And yet a truth, that hour
By him unsung, upon his chords
Descends, their ampler dower.

Of Nature's cyclic life he sang, nor knew
That frailer shape he mourn'd should bloom perpetual too.

VI.

There still—not skilful to retract
A glance as kind as keen—
By the same southern sunset back'd
There still that Maid is seen:
Through song's high grace there stands she! from her eyes
Still beams the cordial mirth, the unshamed surprise!

VII.

Not yet those parted lips remit
A smile that grows and grows:
The Titianic morning yet
Breaks from that cheek of rose:
Still from her locks the breeze its sweetness takes:—
Around her white feet still the ripple fawns and rakes.

VIII.

And, bright'ning in the radiance cast
By her on all around,
That shore lives on, while song may last,
Love-consecrated ground;
Lives like that isthmus, headland half, half isle,
Which smiled to meet Catullus' homeward smile.

IX.

O Sirmio! thou that shedd'st thy fame
O'er old Verona's lake,

Henceforth Varese without blame
Thine honors shall partake:
A Muse hath sung her, on whose front with awe
Thy nymphs had gazed as though great Virtue's self they saw!

X.

What Shape is that, though fair severe,
Which fleets triumphant by
Imaged in yonder mirror clear,
And seeks her native sky,
With locks succinct beneath a threat'ning crest—
Like Juno in the brow, like Pallas in the breast?

XI.

A Muse that flatters nothing base
In man, nor aught infirm,
"Sows the slow olive for a race
Unborn." The destined germ,
The germ alone of Fame she plants, nor cares
What time that secular tree its deathless fruitage bears;

XII.

Pleased rather with her function sage—
To interpret Nature's heart;
The words on Wisdom's sacred page
To wing, through metric art,
With life; and in a chariot of sweet sound
Down-trodden Truth to lift, and waft, the world around.

XIII.

Hail Muse, whose crown, soon won or late,
Is Virtue's, not thine own!
Hail Verse, that tak'st thy strength and state
From Thought's auguster throne!
Varese too would hail thee! Hark that song—
Her almond bowers it thrills and rings her groves along!

October 4, 1856.

LINES WRITTEN NEAR SHELLEY'S HOUSE AT LERICI.

DEDICATED TO J. W. FIELD, ESQ., IN MEMORY OF A DAY PASSED WITH HIM AT LERICI.

I.

AND here he paced! These glimmering pathways strewn
With faded leaves his light swift footsteps crush'd;
The odor of yon pine was o'er him blown:
Music went by him in each wind that brush'd
Those yielding stems of ilex! Here, alone,
He walk'd at noon, or silent stood and hush'd
When the ground-ivy flash'd the moonlight sheen
Back from the forest carpet always green.

II.

Poised as on air the lithe elastic bower
  Now bends, resilient now against the wind
Recoils, like Dryads that one moment cower
  And rise the next with loose locks unconfined.
Through the dim roof like gems the sunbeams shower;
Old cypress trunks the aspiring bay-trees bind,
And soon will have them wholly underneath:
Types eminent of glory conquering death.

III.

Far down upon the shelves and sands below
  The respirations of a southern sea
Beat with susurrent cadence, soft and slow:
  Round the grey cave's fantastic imagery,
In undulation eddying to and fro,
  The purple waves on roll or backward flee;
While, dew'd at each rebound with gentlest shock,
The myrtle leans her green breast on the rock.

IV.

And here he stood; upon his face that light,
  Stream'd from some furthest realm of luminous
      thought,
Which clothed his fragile beauty with the might
  Of suns for ever rising! Here he caught
Visions divine. He saw in fiery flight
  "The hound of Heaven," with heavenly vengeance
      fraught,

"Run down the slanted sunlight of the morn"—*
Prometheus frown on Jove with scorn for scorn.

V.

He saw white Arethusa, leap on leap,
  Plunge from the Acroceraunian ledges bare
With all her torrent streams, while from the steep
  Alpheus bounded on her unaware:
Hellas he saw, a giant fresh from sleep,
  Break from the night of bondage and despair.
Who but had sung as there he stood and smiled
"Justice and truth have found their winged child!"†

VI.

Through cloud and wave and star his insight keen
  Shone clear, and traced a God in each disguise,
Protean, boundless. Like the buskinn'd scene
  All Nature rapt him into ecstasies:
In him, alas! had Reverence equal been
  With Admiration, those resplendent eyes
Had wander'd not through all her range sublime
To miss the one great marvel of all time.

VII.

The winds sang loud; from this Elysian nest
  He rose, and trod yon spine of mountains bleak,
While stormy suns descending in the west
  Stain'd as with blood yon promontory's beak.

* Prometheus Unbound. † Revolt of Islam.

That hour, responsive to his soul's unrest,
  Carrara's marble summits, peak to peak,
Sent forth their thunders like the battle-cry
Of nations arming for the victory.

VIII.

Visions that hour more fair more false he saw
  Than those the mythologic heaven that throng;
Mankind he saw exempt from faith and law,
  Move godlike forth, with science wing'd and song;
He saw the Peoples spurn religious awe,
  Yet tower aloft through inbred virtue strong.
Ah Circe! not for sensualists alone
Thy cup! It dips full oft in Helicon!

IX.

Mankind he saw one equal brotherhood,
  All things in common held as light and air!—
"Vinum demonum!"—Just, and wise, and good—
  Were man all this, such freedom man might bear!
The slave creates the tyrant! In man's blood
  Sin lurks, a panther couchant in his lair.
Nature's confession came before the Creed's;—
Authority is still man's first of needs.

X.

All things in common; equal all; all free!
  Not fancies these, but gifts reserved in trust.
A spiritual growth is Liberty;
  Nature, unnatural made through hate and lust,
Yields it no more or chokes her progeny
  With weeds of foul desire or fell disgust.

Convents have all things common : but on Grace
They rest. Inverted systems lack a base.

XI.

The more obedience to a law divine
  Tempers the chaos of man's heart, the less
Becomes his need of outward discipline
  The balance of injustice to redress.
"Wild Bacchanals of Truth's mysterious wine"*
  Must bear the Mænad's waking bitterness.
Anticipate not heaven. Not great thy worth
Heaven without holiness, and heaven on earth !

XII.

Alas ! the errors thus to truth so near
  That sovereign truths they are, though misapplied,
Errors to pure but passionate natures dear,
  Errors by aspirations glorified,
Errors with radiance crown'd like Lucifer
  Ere fall'n, like him to darkness changed through pride,
These of all errors are the heart and head ;—
The strength of life is theirs ; yet they are dead !

XIII.

That Truth Reveal'd, by thee in madness spurn'd,
  Plato, thy master in the walks of light,
Had knelt to worship ! For its day he yearn'd
  Through the long hungry watches of the night :

* Shelley's Ode to Liberty.

Its dawn in Thought's assumptions he discern'd
  Silvering hoar contemplation's star-loved height;
The God-Man came! Alas! thy phantasy,
A Man-God feigning, storm'd against His sky.

XIV.

Sorrowing for thee, with sorrow joy is mix'd,
  With triumph shame! Our hopes themselves are sad;
But fitful lustres break the shades betwixt;
  So gleams yon olive bower, in mourning clad,
And yet at times with showery gleams transfix'd,
  That opal among trees which grave or glad
Its furtive splendor half reveal'd or wholly
Shoots ever from a base of melancholy.

XV.

Our warfare is in darkness. Friend for foe
  Blindly, and oft with swords exchanged, we strike:
Opinion guesses: Faith alone can know
  Where actual and illusive still are like.
Thine was that strength which fever doth bestow;
  The madness thine of one that, fever-sick,
Beats a sad mother in distemper'd sleep:
Perhaps death woke thee, on her breast to weep!

XVI.

Thee from that Mother sins ancestral tore!—
  No heart hadst thou, from Faith's sole guide remote,
With statutable worship to adore,
  Or learn a nation-licensed Creed by rote;

No heart to snatch thy gloss of sacred lore
  From the blind prophet of the public vote.
Small help from such in life, or when thy pyre
Cast far o'er reddening waves its mirror'd fire!

XVII.

Hark! She thou knew'st not mourns thee! Slowly tolls,
  As sinks the sun, yon church-tower o'er the sea:
Abroad once more the peal funereal rolls,
  And Spezzia now responds to Lerici.
This day is sacred to Departed Souls;
  This day the Dead alone are great; and we
Who live, or seem to live, but live to plead
For the departed myriads at their need.

XVIII.

Behold, the long procession scales the rock;
  In the red glare dusk banners sadly wave!
Behold, the lambs of the immaculate flock
  Fling flowers on noted and on noteless grave!
O Cross! sole Hope that dost not woo to mock!
  Some, some that knew thee not thou liv'st to save—
All spirits not wholly—by their own decree—
From infinite Love exiled, and lost to thee!

All Souls' Day, 1856.

SONNETS.

IRISH COLONIZATION.*

1848.

I.

ENGLAND, thy sinful past hath found thee out!
Washed was the blood-stain from the perfumed hand:
O'er lips self-righteous smiles demure and bland
Flickered, though still thine eye betrayed a doubt,
When round thy palace rose a People's shout—
"Famine makes lean the Helots' helpless land."
What made them Helots? Gibbet, scourge, and brand,
Plaguing with futile rage a Faith devout.
England! six hundred tyrannous years and more,
Trampling a prostrate realm, that strength out-trod,
Which twenty years availed not to restore.
Thou *wert* thy brother's keeper—from the sod
His life-blood crieth. Expiate thou that crime,
Or bear a branded brow throughout all time.

II.

Fell the tall pines!—thou nobler Argo, leap,
Wide-winged deliverer, on the ocean floods;
And westward waft the astonished multitudes

* State assistance to Emigration, if conceded during the Famine years, would have diminished the necessity for that enormous emigration witnessed subsequently to them, while it also diminished the mortality which accompanied the Emigration of those years.

That rot inert, and hideous Sabbath keep;
Or, stung to madness, guiltier ruin heap
  On their own heads. No longer fabled Gods
  Subdue vext waves with tridents and pearl rods;
Yet round that bark heroïc Gods shall sweep,
    And guard an infant Nation. Hope shall flush
With far Hesperean welcome billows hoary:
Valor and virtue, love and joy, and glory,
    A storm-borne Iris, shall before you rush;
And there descending, where your towers shall stand,
Look back, full-faced, and shout, "Britannia, land!"

III.

I heard, in deep prophetic trance immersed,
  The wave, keel-cut, kissing the ship's dark side:—
  Anon men shouted, and the cliffs replied:
O what a vision from the darkness burst!
Europe so fair a city never nursed
  As met me there! It clasped in crescent wide
  The gulf, it crowned the isles, the subject tide
O'er-strode with bridges, and with quays coerced.
In marble from unnumbered mountains robed,
    With altar-shaped Acropolis and crest,
There sat the queenly City, throned and globed:
    Full well that beaming countenance expressed
The soul of a great people. From its eye
Shone forth a second Britain's empery.

IV.

How looks a mother on her babe, a bard
  On some life-labored song? With humble pride,
  And self-less love, and joy to awe allied:—

So should a State that severed self regard,
Her child beyond the waves. Great Nature's ward,
And Time's, that child one day, with God for guide,
Shall waft its parent's image far and wide;
Yea, and its Maker's, if by sin unmarred.
Conquest I deem a vulgar pastime: trade
Shifts like the winds; and power but comes to go:
But this is glorious, o'er the earth to sow
The seed of Nations: darkness to invade
With light: to plant, where silence reigned and death,
The thrones of British law and towers of Christian faith.

V.

England, magnanimous art thou in name:
Magnanimous in nature once thou wert;
But that which ofttimes lags behind desert,
And crowns the dead, as oft survives it—fame.
Can she whose hand a merchant's pen makes tame,
Or sneer of nameless scribe; can she whose heart
In camp or senate still is at the mart,
A Nation's toils, a Nation's honors claim?
Thy shield of old torn Poland twice and thrice
Invoked: thy help as vainly Ireland asks,
Pointing with stark, lean finger, from the crest
Of western cliffs plague-stricken, to the West—
Grey-haired though young. When heat is sucked from ice,
Then shall a Firm discharge a Nation's tasks.

*THE YEAR OF SORROW—IRELAND—*1849.

I.—SPRING.

I.

ONCE more, through God's high will, and grace
Of hours that each its task fulfils,
Heart-healing Spring resumes her place,
The valley throngs and scales the hills;

II.

In vain. From earth's deep heart o'ercharged
The exulting life runs o'er in flowers;
The slave unfed is unenlarged:
In darkness sleep a Nation's powers.

III.

Who knows not Spring? Who doubts, when blows
Her breath, that Spring is come indeed?
The swallow doubts not; nor the rose
That stirs, but wakes not; nor the weed.

IV.

I feel her near, but see her not;
For these with pain uplifted eyes
Fall back repulsed, and vapors blot
The vision of the earth and skies.

V.

I see her not—I feel her near,
  As, charioted in mildest airs,
She sails through yon empyreal sphere,
  And in her arms and bosom bears

VI.

That urn of flowers and lustral dews
  Whose sacred balm, o'er all things shed,
Revives the weak, the old renews,
  And crowns with votive wreaths the dead.

VII.

Once more the cuckoo's call I hear;
  I know, in many a glen profound,
The earliest violets of the year
  Rise up like water from the ground.

VIII.

The thorn I know once more is white;
  And, far down many a forest dale,
The anemones in dubious light
  Are trembling like a bridal veil.

IX.

By streams released that singing flow
  From craggy shelf through sylvan glades
The pale narcissus, well I know,
  Smiles hour by hour on greener shades.

X.

The honeyed cowslip tufts once more
  The golden slopes ; with gradual ray
The primrose stars the rock, and o'er
  The wood-path strews its milky way.

XI.

From ruined huts and holes come forth
  Old men, and look upon the sky!
The Power Divine is on the earth:
  Give thanks to God before ye die!

XII.

And ye, O children worn and weak!
  Who care no more with flowers to play,
Lean on the grass your cold, thin cheek,
  And those slight hands, and whispering, say,

XIII.

"Stern Mother of a race unblest,
  "In promise kindly, cold in deed,—
"Take back, O Earth, into thy breast,
  "The children whom thou wilt not feed."

II.—SUMMER.

I.

APPROVED by works of love and might,
  The Year, consummated and crowned,
Has scaled the zenith's purple height,
  And flings his robe the earth around.

II.

Impassioned stillness—fervors calm—
  Brood, vast and bright, o'er land and deep:
The warrior sleeps beneath the palm;
  The dark-eyed captive guards his sleep.

III.

The Iberian laborer rests from toil;
  Sicilian virgins twine the dance;
Laugh Tuscan vales in wine and oil;
  Fresh laurels flash from brows of France.

IV.

Far off, in regions of the North,
  The hunter drops his winter fur;
Sun-stricken babes their feet stretch forth;
  And nested dormice feebly stir.

V.

But thou, O land of many woes!
  What cheer is thine? Again the breath
Of proved Destruction o'er thee blows,
  And sentenced fields grow black in death.

VI.

In horror of a new despair
  His blood-shot eyes the peasant strains,
With hands clenched fast, and lifted hair,
  Along the daily-darkening plains.

VII.

"Why trusted he to them his store?
"Why feared he not the scourge to come?"
Fool! turn the page of History o'er—
The roll of Statutes—and be dumb!

VIII.

Behold, O People! thou shalt die!
What art thou better than thy sires?
The hunted deer a weeping eye
Turns on his birthplace, and expires.

IX.

Lo! as the closing of a book,
Or statue from its base o'erthrown,
Or blasted wood, or dried-up brook,
Name, race, and nation, thou art gone.

X.

The stranger shall thy hearth possess;
The stranger build upon thy grave·
But know this also—he, not less,
His limit and his term shall have.

XI.

Once more thy volume, open cast,
In thunder forth shall sound thy name;
Thy forest, hot at heart, at last
God's breath shall kindle into flame.

XII.

Thy brook dried up a cloud shall rise,
  And stretch an hourly widening hand,
In God's good vengeance, through the skies,
  And onward o'er the Invader's land.

XIII.

Of thine, one day, a remnant left
  Shall raise o'er earth a Prophet's rod,
And teach the coasts of Faith bereft
  The names of Ireland, and of God.

III.—AUTUMN.

I.

THEN die, thou Year—thy work is done:
  The work ill done is done at last.
Far off, beyond that sinking sun
  Which sets in blood, I hear the blast

II.

That sings thy dirge, and says—"Ascend,
  "And answer make amid thy peers,
(Since all things here must have an end,)
  "Thou latest of the famine years!"

III.

I join that voice. No joy have I
  In all thy purple and thy gold;
Nor in that nine-fold harmony
  From forest on to forest rolled:

IV.

Nor in that stormy western fire,
  Which burns on ocean's gloomy bed,
And hurls, as from a funeral pyre,
  A glare that strikes the mountain's head;

V.

And writes on low-hung clouds its lines
  Of cyphered flame, with hurrying hand;
And flings amid the topmost pines
  That crown the steep, a burning brand.

VI.

Make answer, Year, for all thy dead,
  Who found not rest in hallowed earth;
The widowed wife, the father fled,
  The babe age-stricken from his birth.

VII.

Make answer, Year, for virtue lost;
  For courage proof 'gainst fraud and force
Now waning like a noontide ghost;
  Affections poisoned at their source.

VIII.

The laborer spurned his lying spade;
  The yeoman spurned his useless plough;
The pauper spurned the unwholesome aid,
  Obtruded once, exhausted now.

IX.

The roof-trees fall of hut and hall,
  I hear them fall, and falling cry,
"One fate for each, one fate for all;
  So wills the Law that willed a lie."

X.

Dread power of Man! what spread the waste
  In circles hour by hour more wide,
And would not let the past be past?—
  The Law that promised much, and lied.

XI.

Dread power of God! Whom mortal years
  Nor touch, nor tempt; Who sitt'st sublime
In night of night,—O bid thy spheres
  Resound at last a funeral chime!

XII.

Call up at last the afflicted race,
  Whom man, not God, abolished.—Sore,
For centuries, their strife: the place
  That knew them once shall know no more!

IV.—WINTER.

I.

FALL, snow, and cease not! Flake by flake
  The decent winding-sheet compose.
Thy task is just and pious; make
  An end of blasphemies and woes.

II.

Fall flake by flake ! by thee alone,
  Last friend, the sleeping draught is given :
Kind nurse, by thee the couch is strewn,
  The couch whose covering is from heaven.

III.

Descend and clasp the mountain's crest ;
  Inherit plain and valley deep :
This night on thy maternal breast
  A vanquished nation dies in sleep.

IV.

Lo ! from the starry Temple Gates
  Death rides, and bears the flag of peace :
The combatants he separates ;
  He bids the wrath of ages cease.

V.

Descend, benignant Power ! But O,
  Ye torrents, shake no more the vale :
Dark streams, in silence seaward flow :
  Thou rising storm, remit thy wail.

VI.

Shake not, to-night, the cliffs of Moher,
  Nor Brandon's base, rough sea ! Thou Isle,
The Rite proceeds ! From shore to shore,
  Hold in thy gathered breath the while.

VII.

Fall, snow! in stillness fall, like dew,
  On church's roof and cedar's fan;
And mould thyself on pine and yew;
  And on the awful face of man.

VIII.

Without a sound, without a stir,
  In streets and wolds, on rock and mound,
O, omnipresent Comforter,
  By thee, this night, the lost are found!

IX.

On quaking moor, and mountain moss
  With eyes upstaring at the sky,
And arms extended like a cross,
  The long-expectant sufferers lie.

X.

Bend o'er them, white-robed Acolyte!
  Put forth thine hand from cloud and mist;
And minister the last sad Rite,
  Where altar there is none, nor priest.

XI.

Touch thou the gates of soul and sense;
  Touch darkening eyes and dying ears;
Touch stiffening hands and feet, and thence
  Remove the trace of sins and tears.

XII.

And ere thou seal those filmèd eyes,
  Into God's urn thy fingers dip,
And lay, 'mid eucharistic sighs,
  The sacred wafer on the lip.

XIII.

This night the Absolver issues forth :
  This night the Eternal Victim bleeds :
O winds and woods—O heaven and earth !
  Be still this night. The Rite proceeds !

WIDOWHOOD.

1848.

Not thou alone, but all things fair and good,
Live here bereft, in vestal widowhood,
Or wane in radiant circlet incomplete.
Memory, in widow's weeds, with naked feet,
Stands on a tombstone. Hope, with tearful eyes,
Stares all night long on unillumined skies.
Virtue, an orphan, begs from door to door.
Beside a cold hearth, on a stranger's floor,
Sits exiled Honor. Song, a vacant type,
Hangs on that tree, whose fruitage ne'er was ripe,
Her harp, and bids the casual wind thereon
Lament what might be, fabling what is gone.
Our childhood's world of wonder melts like dew ;

Youth's guardian genius bids our youth adieu ;
And oft the wedded is a widow too.
The best of bridals here is but a troth,—
Only in heaven is ratified the oath :
There, there alone, is clasped in full fruition
  That sacred joy which passed not Eden's gates :
For here the soul is mocked with dream and vision ;
  And outward sense, uniting, separates.
The Bride of Brides, a maid and widow here,
Invokes her Lord, and finds—a Comforter :—
Her loftiest fane is but a visible porch
To sealed Creation's omnipresent Church.

  Zealous that nobler gifts than earth's should live,
Fortune I praise—but praise her, fugitive.
The Roman praised her permanent ;* but we
Have learned her lore (and paid a heavy fee),
Have tracked her promise to its brake of wiles,
And sounded all the shallows of her smiles.
Fortune not gives but sells, and takes instead
A heart made servile, and a discrowned head.
Too soon she comes, and drowns in swamps of sloth
The soul contemplative and active—both ;
Or comes too late, and, with malignant art,
Leaps on the lance that rives the sufferer's heart,
Showering her affluence on a breast supine.
Her best of gifts the usurer's seal and sign
Sustain, and pawn man's life to Destiny.
Ah ! mightier things than man like man can die !

* "Laudo manentem."—HORACE.

Between the ruin and the work half done
I sit: the raw wreck is the sorrier one
Here drops old Desmond's Keep in slow decay:
There the unfinished Mole is washed away.
The moment's fickle promise, and the vast
And consummated greatness,—both are past.
We sink, and none is better for our fall:
We suffer most: but suffering comes to all:
Our sighs but echoes are of earlier sighs;
And in our agonies we plagiarize.
O'er all the earth old States in ruin lie,
And new Ambitions topple from their sky:
Greatness walks lame while clad in mortal mould;
The good are weak—unrighteous are the bold.
Love by Self-love is murdered, or Distrust;
And earth-born Virtue has its "dust to dust."
This Ireland knows. The famine years go by,
And each its ranks of carnage heaps more high:
What voice once manly and what hand once strong
Arraigns, resists, or mitigates the wrong?
The future shall be as the present hour:
The havoc past, again the slaves of Power
Shall boast because once more the harvest waves
In fraudulent brightness o'er a million graves.
Why weep for ties once ours, relaxed or broken?
If weep we must, our tears are all bespoken:
One thing is worthy of them, one alone—
A world's inherent baseness, and our own.

Type of my country, sad, and chaste, and wise!
Forgive the gaze of too regardful eyes:

I saw the black robe and the aspect pale,
And heard in dream that country's dying wail.
Like Night her form arose,—as shades in night
Are lost, thy sorrowing beauty vanished from my
sight.

*THE IRISH GAEL TO THE IRISH NORMAN;**

OR, THE LAST IRISH CONFISCATION.

1850.

YOUR bark in turn is freighted. O'er the seas
You seek a refuge at the Antipodes.
Australia waits you. O my Lord, beware!
Australia! Floats not England's standard there?
Tyrconnell and Tyrone found rest more nigh:
Shrined on Saint Peter's Mount† their ashes lie.
Their cause is mine—and foes, till now, were we;
Now friends, ashamed were I thy shame to see.
Has Ruin no decorum? Grief no sense?
Shall England house thee? England drives thee
hence!

* Toward the end of the Irish Famine many estates were precipitated on the market and sold for half their value, owing to a course of legislation which their proprietors denounced as confiscation. This poem was written on hearing that a nobleman thus suddenly reduced to ruin was about to emigrate to Australia. It is dramatic in its scope, and represents the feelings with which the descendant of some great House dispossessed in old times might contemplate the ruin of one belonging to the later Race.

† San Pietro in Montorio.

O worker of thy sorrows, with a vow
Bind thou that head reduced, and careful brow,
Wholly to root that idol from thy heart:
Swear that thy race never shall have a part
In aught that England boasts, achieves, confers:
Her past is thine—thy future is not hers.

Loosed from the agony of fruitless strife
You stand, a lost man 'mid the wreck of life,
And round you gaze. Sad Eva also gazed
All round that bridal field of blood, amazed;—
Spoused to new fortunes. But your head is gray!
Beyond your castle droops the dying day;
And, drifting down loose gusts of wailing wind,
Night comes, with rain before and frost behind.
Lean men that groped for sea-weeds on the shore
All day, now hide in holes on fen and moor.
The cliffs lean forth their brows to meet the scourge
Of blast on blast: around their base the surge
Welters in shades from iron headlands thrown:
Through chasm and cave subaqueous thunders moan—
That sound thou lov'st! Once more the Desmonds fall:
To-night old Wrongs shake hands in History's hall;
And, clashing through responsive vaults of Time,
Old peals funereal marry chime to chime.
Of such no more! Beside your fireless hearth
Sit one night yet: and, moody or in mirth,
Compare the past and present, and record
The fortunes of your Order in a word.
England first used, then spurned it! Hour by hour,
For centuries her laws, her fame, her power

Hung on its hand. It gloried to sustain,
High o'er the clouds that sweep the Atlantic main,
The banner with her blazonries enrolled:
Then came the change, and ye were bought and sold:
Then came the change, and ye received your due.
Sir, to your country had ye proved as true
As to your England, she had held by you:
Ruin ye might have proved; ye might have known
Even then, the scorn of others—not your own!

Pardon hard words. Your Race, not mine, is hard:
But wounds and work the hand too soft have scarred:
We are your elders—first-born in distress;
And century-seasoned woes grow pitiless.
Hierarchs are we in pain, where ye but learn:
We have an Unction, and our Rite is stern.
If on our brows still hang ancestral glooms,
Forgive the children of the Catacombs.
What have the dead to do with love or ruth?
I died; and live once more—I live for Truth:
Hope and delusion trouble me no more:
Therefore, expatriate on my native shore,
Anguish and doubt shake other nerves, not mine:
I drop no tear into the bitter brine:
The world in which I move is masculine.

Why to Australia? Britain too was dear—
Must, then, the Britain of the southern sphere
Rack you in turn? Seek you once more to prove
The furies of a scorned, unnatural love
That cleaves to insult, and on injury feeds,
And, upon both cheeks stricken, burns and bleeds?

Son of the North, why seek you not once more
The coasts where sang the warrior Scald of yore?
If unhistoric regions you must tread,
Hallowed by no communion with the dead,
Never by saint, or sage, or hero trod;
Where never lifted fane upraised to God
In turn, the hearts of sequent generations,
Where never manly races rose to nations,
Marshalled by knightly arm or kingly eye;
If, with new fortunes, a new earth you try,
Then seek, oh, seek her in her purity!
Drain not civilization's dregs and lees.
In many an island clipt by tropic seas,
Nature keeps yet a race by arts untamed,
Who live half-innocent and unashamed.
Ambition frets not them. In regions calm,
'Mid prairies vast, or under banks of palm,
They sing light wars and unafflicting loves,
And vanish as the echo leaves the groves!
Smooth space divides their cradles and their graves.
What are they? Apparitions—casual waves
Heaved up in life's successive harmony!
Brief smiles of nature followed by a sigh!
Why not with such abide awhile and die?

O, summoned are thy death to that repose
The grave concedes to others! by thy foes
Franchised with that which friendship never gave—
A heart as free from tremors as the grave!
Last of a race whose helm and lance were known
In furthest lands—now exiled from thine own—

Give thanks! How many a sight is spared to thee,
Which we, thy sires in suffering, saw and see!
Thou hast beheld thy country, by the shocks
Of three long winters, driven upon the rocks
High and more high. Thou shalt not, day by day,
See her dismembered planks, the wrecker's prey,
Abused without remorse to uses base:
Thou hast beheld the home of all thy race,
Their lawns, their walks, and every grove and stream—
Their very tombs—pass from thee like a dream,
And leave thee bare. But thou shalt not behold
Thy woods devastated, nor gathering mould
Subdue the arms high hung, and blight the bloom
Of pomps heraldic, redd'ning scroll and tomb;
Nor the starred azure touched by mists cold-lipped,
Till choir and aisle are black as vault and crypt,
Nor from the blazoned missal wane and faint
The golden age of martyr, maid, and saint,
Umbria's high pathos, and the Tuscan might,
And all thy wondering childhood's world of light.
Thou shalt not see that Cross thou loved'st so well
From minster towers rock-built, and hermit's cell
Swept by the self-same blast that sent the hind
Shivering to caves, and struck a kingdom blind!
All that was thine, while seas between thee roll
And them, in some still cloister of thy soul
Shall live, as, in a mother's heart inisled,
Lives on the painless memory of a child
Buried a babe. One image all shall make
Still as the gleam of sunset-lighted lake

Kenned from a tower o'er leagues of wood and lawn ;
Or as perchance our planet looks, withdrawn
From some pure spirit that leaves her—to his sight
Lessening, not lost—a disk of narrowing light
Sole-hung in regions of pure space afar—
Of old the world he lived in, now a star !

But the wind swells yon sails. Why waste we breath ?
My Lord, for thy soul's sake, and a good death,
Forget the things a Gael's unmannered pen
For thee records not, but for later men.
Since hope is gone, let peace be thine instead.
The snows which heap too soon that Norman head,
Should calm it ; and a heart that bleeds for aye
Has less to lose, and less to feel, each day.
Seek not thy joys when on the desolate shore
The raked rocks thunder, and the caverns roar,
And the woods moan, while shoots the setting sun
Discords of angry lights o'er billows dun.
Make white thy thoughts as is a Vestal's sleep—
Bloodless : prolong, beside the murmuring deep,
Thy matutinal slumbers, till the bird
That tuned, not broke them, is no longer heard.
The flowers the children of the Stranger bring
Indulgent take : permit thy latest Spring
To lure from thee all bitterness and wrath :
Into Death's bosom, genial as a bath,
Sink back absolved. Justice to God belongs :
Soul latest-stricken, leave with Him thy wrongs !

Justice, o'er angels and o'er men supreme,
Still in mid heaven sustains her balanced beam,

With whose vast scales, whether they sink or rise,
The poles of earth are forced to sympathize.
Unseen she rules, wrapped round in cloud and awe;
Her silence is the seal of mortal law;
Her voice the harmony of every sphere:
Most distant is she ever, yet most near;
Most strong when least regarded. From her eyes
That light goes forth which cheers the brave and
wise;
And in the arm that lifts aloft her sword,
Whatever might abides on earth is stored.
Fret not thyself. Watch thou (and wait) her hand!
The thunder-drops fall fast. In every land
Humanity breathes quick, and coming storm
Looks through man's soul with flashes swift and
warm:
The fiery trial and the shaken sieve
Shall prove the nations. What can live shall live.
Falsehood shall die; and falsehoods widest-based
Shall lie the lowest, though they fall the last.

Down from the mountain of their greatness hurled,
What witness bear the Nations to the World?
Down rolled, like rocks along the Alpine stairs,
What warning voice is theirs, and ever theirs?
Their ears the Nations unsubverted close,
For who would hear the voice whose words are
Woes?
Woe to ancestral greatness, if the dower
Of knightly worth confirm no more its power.
Woe to commercial strength, if sensual greed
Heap up like waves its insolent gold, nor heed

What solid good rewards the poor man's toil.
Woe to the Monarch, if the unholy oil
Of smooth-tongued flattery be his balm and chrism.
Woe to the State cleft through by social schism.
Woe to Religion, when the birds obscene
Of Heresy from porch to altar-screen
Range free; while from the temple-eaves look down
Doubt's shadowy brood, ill-masked in cowl or gown.
Woe to the Rulers by the People ruled—
A People drowned in sense, and pride-befooled,
Trampling where sages once, and martyrs, trod.
Ye nations meet your doom, or serve at last your
God!

IRELAND. 1851.

O THOU! afflicted and beloved, O Thou!
Who on thy wasted hands and bleeding brow—
Dread miracle of Love—from reign to reign,
Freshenest thy stigmata of sacred Pain:
Lamp of the North when half the world was night;
Now England's darkness 'mid her noon of light;
History's sad wonder, whom all lands save one
Gaze on through tears, and name with gentler tone:
O Tree of God! that burnest unconsumed;
O Life in Death! for centuries entombed;
That art uprisen, and higher far shalt rise,
Drawn up by strong attraction to the skies:
Thyself most weak, yet strengthened from above:
Smitten of God, yet not in hate, but love:—

Thy love make perfect, and from love's pure hate
The earthlier scum and airier froth rebate !
Be strong ; be true ! Thy palms not yet are won :
Thine ampler mission is but now begun.
Hope not for any crown save that thou wearest—
The crown of thorns. Preach thou that Cross thou
bearest !
Go forth ! each coast shall glow beneath thy tread !
What radiance bursts from heaven upon thy head ?
What fiery pillar is before thee borne ?
Thy loved and lost ! They lead thee to thy morn !
They pave thy paths with light ! Beheld by man,
Thou walkest a shade, not shape, beneath a ban.
Walk on—work on—love on ; and, suffering, cry,
" Give me more suffering, Lord, or else I die."

THE SISTERS; OR, WEAL IN WOE.

AN IRISH TALE.

DEDICATED TO STEPHEN SPRING RICE.

From nine to twelve my guest was eloquent
In anger, mixed with sorrow, at the things
He saw around us—lands half marsh, half weeds,
Gates from the gate-posts miserably divorced,
Hovels ill-thatch'd, wild fences, fissured roads—
"Your people never for the future plan ;
They live but for the moment." Thus he spake,
A youth just entering on his broad domains,

A senator in prorogation time
Travelling for knowledge, Oxford's accurate scholar,
A perfect rider, clean in all his ways,
But by traditions narrow'd. As the moon
Turns but one side to earth, so show'd that world
Whereon he gazed, for stubborn was his will,
And Ireland he had never loved. "You err,"
I answer'd, taking in good part his wrath,
"Our peasant too has prescience; far he sees;
Earth is his foreground only, rough or smooth;
In him from seriousness the lightness comes:
Too serious is he to make sacrifice
For fleeting good; the battles of this world
He with the left hand fights, and half in sport;
He has his moment—and eternity."
"Ay, ay," exclaim'd my guest, "your Church, she does it!
Your feasts and fasts and wakes and social rites,
With 'Sir,' and 'Ma'am,' and usages of Court:—
I've seen a hundred men leave plough and spade
To take a three weeks' infant to its grave,
A cripple pay two shillings for a cart
To bear him to the Holy Well—Sick Land!
Look up! the proof is round you written large!
Your Faith is in the balance wanting found:
Your shipless seas confess it; bridgeless streams;
Your wasted wealth of ore, and moor, and bay!
Beneath the Upas shade of Faith depraved
All things lie dead — wealth, comfort, freedom, power—
All that great Nations boast!" "Such things," I answer'd,

The Gentiles seek; and you new texts have found:
'Ecclesiæ stantis vel cadentis,' friend;—
'Blessed the rich: blessed whom all men praise:'
New Scriptures, these; the Irish keep the old!
Say, are there not diversities of gifts?
Are there not virtues—Industry is one—
Which reap on earth, whilst others sow for heaven?
Faith, hope, and love, and purity, and patience,
Humility, and self-forgetfulness,
These too are virtues; yet they rear not States.
What then? Of many Nations earth is made:
Each hath its function; each its part for others:
If all were hand, where then were ear or eye?
If all were foot, where head? You rail, my friend,
Not at my country only but your own.
The land that gave us birth our service claims,
The suffering land our love. Yet England, too,
They love, and they the most, who flatter not.
A thousand years of nobleness she lived
Whereof you rob her! In this isle are men
By ancient lineage hers. Such men might say,
'My England was entomb'd ere yours had birth'—
Dates she from Arkwright only? Rose the Nation
With Alfred, or those Tudor Kings who built
The Golden Gate of England's modern time,
But built it upon liberties annull'd,
Old glories quench'd, the old nobles dead or quell'd—
Aye, wrecks more sad?" His host, I could not use
Words rough as his albeit to shield a land
For every shaft a targe; so changed the theme
To her he knew—thence loved.

He loved his country;

An older man than he for things less great
Had loved her less. Yet who could gaze, unmoved,
From Windsor's terraced heights o'er those broad
meads
Lit by the pomp of silver-winding Thames
Dropping past templed grove, and hall, and farm,
Toward the great City? Who, unthrill'd, could mark
Her Minsters, towering far away, with heads
That stay the sunset of old times; or them,
Oxford and Cambridge, England's anchors twain,
That to her moorings hold her? Fresh from these
Who, who could tread, O Wye, thy watery vale
Where Tintern reigns in ruin; who could rest
Where Bolton finds in Wharf a warbling choir,
Or where the sea-wind fans thy brow discrown'd,
Furness, nor love and wonder? Who, untouch'd,
When evening creeps from Scawfell toward Black
Combe,
Could wander by thy darkly gleaming lakes
Embay'd mid sylvan garniture and isles
From saint or anchoret named, within the embrace
Of rural mountains green, or sound, scent, touch,
Of kine-besprinkled, soft, partition'd vales,
Almost domestic? Shadow-haunted land!
By Southey's lake Saint Herbert holds his own!
The knightly armor now by Yew-dale's crag
Rings loud no longer: Grasmere's reddening glass
Reflects no more the on-rushing clan; yet still
Thy Saxon kings, and ever-virgin Queens
Possess thee with a quiet pathos; still,
Like tarnish'd path forlorn of moon that sets
Over wide-water'd moor and marsh, thy Past

A spiritual sceptre, though deposed, extends
From sea to sea—from century-worn St. Bees
To Cuthbert's tomb under those eastern towers
On Durham's bowery steep!
He loved his country:
That love I honor'd. Great and strong he call'd her;
But well I knew that had her greatness waned,
His love had wax'd.
As thus we talk'd the sun
Launch'd through the hurrying clouds a rainy beam
That smote the hills. My guest exclaim'd, "Come forth—
We waste the day! Yon ridge my fancy takes;
Climb we its crest!" The wolf-hound at our feet,
Our drift divining, bounded sudden on us
In rapture of prospective gratitude.

We pass'd the offending gate; a plank for bridge,
We pass'd the offending stream which dash'd its spray
Contemptuous on us, proud of liberty.
I laugh'd.—"Our passionate Ireland is the stream;
Seven hundred years at will it mocks or chides;
You have not made it turn your English mill!"
We scaled the hills; we push'd through miles of trees,
Which, sire and son, had held their own since first
The tall elk trod their ways. Lightning and storm
Had left large wrecks:—election wars, not less,
Or hospitalities as fierce, when home
A thousand chiefless clansmen dragg'd the bride,
Or danced around a cradle,—ah, brave hearts!
Loyal where cause for loyalty was scant!

Vast were those woods and fair; rock, oak, and yew,
Grey, green, and black, in varying measures striking
That three-string'd lyre which charms not ear but eye.
Long climbing, from the woodland we emerged
And paced a rocky neck of pale green pasture,
The limit of two counties. Full in face
Rush'd, ocean-scented, the harmonic wind:
Round us the sheep-bells chimed; a shower late past
With jewelry had hung the blackberry bush,
And gorse-brake half in gold. On either side
Thin-skinn'd, ascetic, slippery, the descent
Down slanted toward the creeping mists. Our goal
We reach'd at last—a broad and rocky mass
Forth leaning, lordly, unto lands remote,
The lion's head of all those feebler hills
That cowering slunk behind it. Far around
Low down, subjected, stretch'd the sea-like waste
Shade-swept, unbounded, like infinity.
An hour before his time the sun had dropp'd
Behind a mountain-wall of barrier cloud
Wide as the world: but five great beams converged
Toward the invisible seat of his eclipse;
And over many a river, bay, and mere
Lay the dull red of ante-dated eve.

That summit was a churchyard. Cross-engraven
Throng'd the close tomb-stones. Each one prayed for peace;
And some were raised by men whose heads were white
Ere selfless toil had won the hoarded coins
That honor'd thus a parent. In the midst

A tomb-like chapel, thirty feet by ten,
Stood monumental, with stone roof and walls
The wrestling centuries slid from. Nigh we sat,
While, by the polish'd angle split, the wind
Hiss'd like a forkèd serpent. Silent long
My friend remain'd; his sallies all had ceased,
A man of tender nerve though stubborn thought.
The scene weigh'd on him like a Prophet's scroll
Troubling some unjust City. Round and round
He scann'd the desolate region, and at last
Pray'd me the hieroglyphic to expound.
"Yon tower which blurs the lonely lake far off,
What is it?" And I answer'd, "Know you not?
He built it, he that Norman horsed and mail'd,
Who, strong in Henry's might and Adrian's bull,
Rent from the Gaelic monarch half his realm;—
The rest came later, dowry of the bride."

Once more he mused; then, westward pointing, spake:—
"Yon lovely hills, yet low, with Phidian line,
That melt into the horizon:—on their curve
A ruined castle stands; the sky glares through it,
Red, like a conflagration?" I replied:
"Four hundred years the Norman held his own;
He spake the People's language; they in turn
His war-cry had resounded far and wide;
Their history he had grown, impersonate.
The Land rejoiced in him, and of his greatness
Uplifted, glorying, on a neck high held
The beautiful burden, as the wild stag lifts
O'er rocky Torc his antlers! Would you more?

The Desmond was unloved beside the Thames;
The right of the great Palatine was trampled;
His Faith by law proscribed. O'er tombs defaced,
In old Askeaton's Abbey, of his sires
He vow'd unwilling war. Long years the realm
Reel'd like a drunken man. Behold the end!
Yon wreck speaks all!"

Thus question after question
Dragg'd, maim'd and mangled, dragg'd reluctant forth
Time's dread confession! Crime replied to crime:
Whom Tudor planted Cromwell rooted out;
For Charles they fought;—to fight for Kings, their spoilers,
The rebel named rebellion! William next!
Once more the Nobles were down hurl'd; once more
Nobility as in commission placed
By God among the lowly. Loyalty
To native Princes, or to Norman chiefs,
Their lawless conquerors, or to British Kings,
Or her the Mother Church that ne'er betray'd,
Had met the same reward. The legend spake
Words few but plain, grim rubric traced in blood;
While, like a Fury fleeting through the air,
History from all the octaves of her lyre
Struck but one note! What rifted tower and keep
Witness'd of tyrannous and relentless wars,
That shipless gulfs, that bridgeless streams and moors,
Black as if lightning-scarr'd, or curst of God,
Proclaim'd of laws blacker than brand or blight—
Those Penal Laws. The tale was none of mine;

Stone rail'd at stone; grey ruins dumbly frown'd
Defiance, and the ruin-handled blast
Scatter'd the fragments of Cassandra's curse
From the far mountains to the tombs close by,
Which mutter'd treason.

That sad scene to me
Had lost by use its pathos as the scent
Which thrills us, while we pass the garden, palls
On one within it tarrying. To my friend
It spake its natural language: and as he
Who, hard through habit, reads with voice unmoved
A ballad that once touch'd him, if perchance
Some listener weeps, partakes that listener's trouble,
Even so the stranger's sorrow struck on mine,
And I believed the things which I beheld,
There sitting silent. When at last he spake,
The spirit of the man in part was changed;
The things but heard of he had seen: the truths
Coldly conceded now he realized:
Justice at last, with terrible recoil,
Leap'd up full-arm'd, a strong man after sleep,
And dash'd itself against the wrong! I answer'd:
"Once more you speak the words you spake this morn,—
'Look up, the proof is round you, written large:'
But in an alter'd sense."

I spake, and left him:
Left him to seek a tomb which three long years
Holds one I honor'd. Half-an-hour went by;

Then he rejoin'd me. With a knitted brow,
And clear vindictiveness of speech, like him
Who, loving, hates the sin of whom he loves,
He spake against the men who, having won
By right or wrong the mastery of this isle
(For in our annals he was versed, nor ran
In custom's blinkers, save on modern roads),
Could make of it, seven hundred years gone by,
No more than this !—Then I :—" No country loved
they :
Her least, the imperial realm !—'Tis late to mourn ;
Let past be past." " The Past," he said, " is pre-
sent ;
And o'er the Future stretches far a hand
Shadowy and minatory." " Come what may,"
I said, " no suffering can to us be new ;
No shadow fail to dew some soul with grace.
The history of a Soul holds in it more
Than doth a Nation's ! In its every chance
Eternity lies hid ; from every step
Branch forth two paths piercing infinity.
These things look noblest from their spiritual side :
A statesman, on the secular side you see them,
And doubt a future based on such a past.
'Tis true, with wrong dies not the effect of wrong,
Or sense thereof :—'tis true stern Power with time
Changes its modes, not instinct : true it is
That hollow peace is war that wears a mask :
Yet let us quell to-day unquiet thoughts :
She rests who lies in yonder tomb : sore pains
She suffer'd : yet within her there was peace :
In God's high Will she rests, and why not we ?"

Thus we conversed till twilight, thickening, crept,
Compassionate, o'er a scene to which we said
Twilight seem'd native, day a garish vest
Worn by a slave. Returning, oft my friend
Cast loose, in wrath, the arch-rebel Truth ; I answer'd :
"She rests, and why not we ? O suffering land !
Thee, too, God shields ; and only for this cause
Can they that love thee sleep." Her tale at last
He sought with instance. 'Twas not marvellous,
I told him : yet to calm his thoughts perturb'd,
Thus, while the broad moon o'er the lonely moor
Rose, blanching as she soar'd, till pools, at first
With trembling light o'erlaid, gave back her face,
And all the woodland waves as eve advanced
Shone bright o'er sombre hollows, I recounted
The fragments of a noteless Irish life,
Not strange esteem'd among us. Such a theme
I sought not. Ill it were to forge for friend
A providence, or snare him though to Truth.
Yet I was pleased he sought that tale. 'Twas sad
But in its dusky glass (and this I hid not)
Shadow'd a phantom image of my country,
Vanquish'd yet victor, in her weal and woe.

The Father in the prime of manhood died ;
The mother follow'd soon ; their children twain,
Margaret Mac Carthy, and her sister Mary,
The eldest scarcely ten years old, survived
To spread cold hands upon a close-seal'd grave,
And cry to those who answer'd not. The man

Who, in that narrow spot to them the world,
Stood up and seem'd as God ;—that gentler one
Who overhung like Heaven their earliest thought,
And in the bosom of whose sleepless love
Reborn they seem'd each morning—both were dead.
In grief's bewilderment the orphans stood
Like one by fraud betray'd : nor moon, nor sun,
Nor trees, nor grass, nor herds, nor hills appear'd
To them what they had been. In sadden'd eyes,
Frighten'd yet dull, in voice subdued, and feet
That moved as though they fear'd to wake the dead,
Men saw that nowhere loneliness more lives
Than in the breasts of children. Time went by ;
The farm was lost ; and to her own small home
Their father's mother led them. 'Twas not far ;
They could behold the orchard they had loved ;
Behind the hedge could hear the robin sing,
And the bees murmur. Slowly, as the trance
Of grief dissolved, the present lived once more ;
The past became a dream !

I see them still !
Softly the beauty-making years on went,
And each one as he pass'd our planet's verge
Look'd back, and left a gift. A darker shade
Dropp'd on the deepening hair ; a brighter gleam
Forth flash'd from sea-blue eyes with darkness fringed.
Like, each to each, their stature growing kept
Unchanged gradation. To her grandmother
A quick eye, and a serviceable hand
Endear'd the elder most ; she kept the house ;
Hers was the rosier cheek, the livelier mind,

The smile of readier cheer. In Mary lived
A visionary and pathetic grace
Through all her form diffused, from those small feet
Up to that beauteous-shaped and netted head,
Which from the slender shoulders and slight bust
Rose like a queen's. Alone, not solitary,
Full often half an autumn day she sat
On the high grass-banks, foot with foot enclasped,
Now twisting osiers, watching cloud-shades now,
Or rushing vapors, through whose chasms there shone
Far off an alien race of clouds like Alps
O'er Courmayeur white-gleaming, and like them
To stillness frozen. Well that orphan knew them,
Those marvellous clouds that roof our Irish wastes;
Spring's lightsome veil outblown, sad Autumn's bier,
And Winter's pillar of electric light
Slanted from heaven. A spirit-world, so seem'd it,
In them was imaged forth to her.

With us
The childish heart betroths itself full oft
In vehement friendship. Mary's was of these;
And thus her fancy found that counterweight
Which kept her feet on earth. With her there walk'd
Two years a little maiden of the place,
Her comrade, as men call'd her. Eve by eve
Homeward from school we saw them as they pass'd,
One arm of each about the other's neck,
Above both heads a single cloak. She died,
To Mary leaving what she valued most,
A rosary strung with beads from Olivet.
Daily did Mary count those beads:—from each
The picture of some Christian Truth ascending,

Till all the radiant Mysteries shone on high
Like constellations, and man's gloomy life
For her to music roll'd on poles of love
Through realms of glory. Hope makes Love immortal!
That friend she ne'er forgot. In later years
Working with other maidens equal-aged,
(A lady of the land instructed them,)
In circle on the grass, not them she saw,
Heard not the song they sang: alone she sat,
And heard 'mid sighing pines and murmuring streams
The voice of the departed.
Smoothly flow'd
Till Margaret had attain'd her eighteenth year
The tenor of their lives; and they became,
Those sisters twain, a name in all the vale
For beauty, kindness, truth, for modest grace,
And all that makes that fairest flower of all
Earth bears, heaven fosters—peasant nobleness:—
For industry the elder. Mary fail'd
In this, a dreamer; indolence her fault,
And self-indulgence, not that coarser sort
Which seeks delight, but that which shuns annoy.
And yet she did her best. The dull red morn
Shone, beamless, through the wintry hedge while pass'd
That pair with panniers, or, on whitest brows,
The balanced milk-pails. Margaret ruled serene,
A wire-fenced empire smiling through soft glooms,
The pure, health-breathing dairy. Softer hand
Than Mary's ne'er let loose the wool; no eye
Finer pursued the on-flowing line: her wheel

Murmur'd complacent joy like kitten pleased.
With us such days abide not.
Sudden fell
Famine, the Terror never absent long,
Upon our land. It shrank—the daily dole;
The oatmeal trickled from a tighter grasp;
Hunger grew wild through panic; infant cries
Madden'd at times the gentle into wrong:
Death's gentleness more oft for death made way;
And like a lamb that openeth not its mouth
The sacrificial People, fillet-bound,
Stood up to die. Amid inviolate herds
Thousands the sacraments of death received,
Then waited God's decree. These things are known:
Strangers have witness'd to them; strangers writ
The epitaph again and yet again.
The nettles and the weeds by the way-side
Men ate: from sharpening features and sunk eyes
Hunger glared forth, a wolf more lean each hour;
Children seem'd pigmies shrivell'd to sudden age;
And the deserted babe too weak to wail
But shook if hands, pitying or curious, raised
The rag across him thrown. In England alms
From many a private hearth were largely sent,
As ofttimes they have been. 'Twas vain. The land
Wept while her sons sank back into her graves
Like drowners 'mid still seas. Who could escaped:
And on a ghost-throng'd deck, amid such cries
As from the battle-field ascend at night
When stumbling widows grope o'er heaps of slain,
Amid such cries stood Mary, when the ship
Its cable slipp'd and, on the populous quays

Grating, without a wind, on the slow tide,
Dropp'd downward to the main.
For western shores
Those emigrants were bound. At Liverpool,
Fann'd by the ocean breeze, the smouldering fire
Of fever burst into a sudden flame ;
The stricken there were left ;—among them Mary.
How long she knew not in an hospital
She lay, a Babel of confused distress
Dinn'd with delirious strife. But o'er her brow
God shook the dew of dreams wherein she trod
The shadow'd wood-walks of old days once more,
And dabbled in old streams. Ere long, still weak,
Abroad she roam'd, a basket on her arm,
With violets heap'd. The watchman of the city
Laid his strong hand upon her drooping head
Banning the impostor. 'Twas her rags, she thought,
Incensed him, and in meekness moved she on.
When one with lubrique smile toy'd with her flowers,
And spake of violet eyes and easier life,
She understood not, but misliked, and pass'd.
In Liverpool an aged priest she found,
A kinsman of her mother's. Much to her
Of emigrants he spake, and of their trials,
Old ties annull'd, and 'mid temptations strange
Lacking full oft the Bread of Life. She wept ;
Before the tabernacle's lamp she pray'd
Freshly-absolved and heavenliest, with a prayer
That shower'd God's blessing o'er the wanderers down ;
But dead was her desire to cross the main.
Her strength restored, beyond the city-bound
With others of her nation she abode,

Amid the gardens laboring. A rough clan
Those outcasts seem'd ; not like their race at home :
Nor chapel theirs, nor school. Their strength was
prized ;
Themselves were so esteem'd as that sad tribe
Beside the Babylonian streams that wept,
By those that loved not Sion.
Weeks grew months ;
And, with the strength to suffer, sorrow came.
Hard by their nomad camp a youth there lived
Of wealthier sort, who look'd upon this maid :
Her country was his own : he loved it not ;
Had rooted quickly in the stranger's land ;
And versatile, cordial, specious, seeming-frank,
Contracting for himself a separate peace,
Had prosper'd, but had prosper'd in such sort
As they that starve within. Her confidence
He gain'd. To love unworthy, still he loved her :
Loved with the love of an unloving heart—
That love which either is in shallows lost,
Or in its black depth breeds the poison weed.
She knew him not ; how could she ? He himself
Knew scantly. Near her what was best within him
Her golden smile sunn'd forth ; but, dark and cold,
Like a benighted hemisphere abode
A moiety of his being which she saw not.
His was a superficial nature, vain,
And hard, to good impressions sensitive,
And most admiring virtues least his own ;
A mirror that took in a seeming world,
And yet remain'd blank surface. He was crafty,
Follow'd the plough with diplomatic heart ;

His acts were still like the knight's move at chess,
Each a surprise ; not less, to nature's self
Who heard him still referr'd them. "What !" men said,
"Marry the portionless !" Strange are fortune's freaks !
The wedding-day was fix'd, the ring brought home,
When from a distant uncle tidings came :
His latest son was dead. "Take thou my farm,
And share my house "—So spake the stern old man—
"And wed the wife whom I for thee have found."
He show'd the maid that letter. Slowly the weeds
Made way adown the thick and stifled stream,
And others follow'd ; slowly sailed the cloud
Through the dull sky, and others followed slowly :
At last he spake. Low were his words and thin,
Many, but scarcely heard. He asked—her counsel !
Her cheek one moment burn'd. Death-cold, once more
A little while she sat ; then rose and said :—
"You would be free ; I free you ; go in peace."
'Twas the good angel in his heart that loved her ;
'Twas not the man himself ! He wept, but went.
The woman of the house that night was sure
The girl had loved him not. She thought not so
When, four months past, she mark'd her mouth, aside,
Tremble, his name but utter'd.
Sharp the wrong !
Yet they on Life's bewildered book would force
A partial gloss it bears not who assume
The injured wholly free from blame. The world
Is not a board in squares of black and white,
Or else the judgment-executing tongue
Would lack probation. Wrong'd men are not angels ;
Wrong's chiefest sin is this—it genders wrong ;

So stands the offender in his own esteem
Exculpate ; while the feebly-judging starve
The just cause, babbling " mutual was the offence !"
—The man was weak ; not wholly vile. 'Twas well,
Doubtless, to free him ; yet in after years,
When early blight had struck his radiant head,
The girl bewail'd the pride that left thus tempted
The man she loved ; arraign'd the wrath that left him
Almost without farewell. His letter too,
Unopen'd she return'd. 'Twas strange ! so sweet—
Not less there lived within her, down, far down,
A fire-spring seldom waken'd ! When a child
At times, by some strange jealousy disturb'd
From her still dream she flash'd in passion quell'd
Ere from her staider sister's large blue eyes
The astonishment had pass'd. Such moods remain'd
Though rare—that wrath of tender hearts, which scorns
Revenge, which scarcely utters its complaint,
And yet forgives but slowly.
In those days
Within the maiden's bosom there arose
Sea-longings, and desire to sail away
She knew not whither ; and her arms she spread,
Weeping, to winds and waves, and shores unknown,
Lighted by other skies ; and inly thus
She reason'd, self-deceived. " What keeps thee here ?
" 'Twas for a farther bourne thou bad'st farewell
" To those at home, and here thou art as one
" That hangs between two callings." In her heart
Tempests low-toned to ocean-tempests yearn'd,
And ever when she mark'd the shipmast forest
That on the smoky river swayed far off,

Her wish became a craving. Soon once more
Alone 'mid hundreds on a rain-wash'd deck
She stood, and saw the billows heave around,
And all the passions of that headlong world.
Dark-visaged ocean frown'd with hoary brows
Against dark skies; huge, lumbering water-weights
Went shouldering through the abysses: streaming clouds
Ran on the lower levels of the wind;
And in the universe of things she seem'd
An atom random blown. Full many a morn
Rose red through mists, like babe that weeps to rise;
Full many an evening died from wave to wave;—
Then gradual peace possess'd her. Love may wound,
But 'tis self-love that wound exasperates;
A noble nature casts out bitterness,
And o'er the scar, like pine-tree incorrupt,
Weeps healing gums. Heart-whole she gazed at last,
On the great city chiefest of that realm
Which wears the Future's glory. Landed, soon
Back to old duties with a mightier zest
Her heart, its weakening sadness pass'd, return'd;
Kindness made service easier; and the tasks
At first distasteful, smiled on her ere long.
There she was loved once more; there all went well;
And there in peace she might have lived and died;
Yet in that region she abode not long.
In part a wayward instinct drave her forth;
In part a will that from the accomplish'd end
Unstable swerved; in part a hope forlorn.
A site she sought, their sojourn who had left
Long since her village. There old names, old voices,

Faces unknown, yet recognized, throng'd round her
In unconsummate union, (hearts still like,
Yet all beside so different,) not like Souls
Re-met in heaven—more like those Shades antique
That, 'mid the empurpled fields, of other airs
Mindful, in silence trod the lordly land,
Or flock'd around the latest guest of Death
With question sad of home. Imperfect ties
Rub severance into soreness. Mary pass'd,
Thus urged, ere long to lonelier climes. She track'd
Companion'd sometimes, sometimes without friend,
The boundless prairie, sail'd the sea-like lake,
Descended the broad river as it rush'd
Through immemorial forests: lastly stood
Sole, 'mid that city by the southern sea.

There sickness fell upon her: there her hand
Dropt, heavier daily, on her task half done;
Her feet wore chains unseen. The end, she thought,
Was coming. Ofttimes, in her happier days,
She wish'd to die and be with God: yet now,
Wearied by many griefs, to life she clung,
Upbraiding things foregone and inly sighing
"None loves to die." Sorrow, earth-born, in some
Breeds first the Earth-infection; in them works,
Like those pomegranate seeds that barr'd from light
For aye sad Ceres' child! Alas! how many,
The ill-honor'd ecstacies of youth surceased,
Exchange its clear spring for the mire! Hope sick,
How oft Faith dies! How few are they in whom
Virgin but yields to Vestal; casual pureness
Merged in essential; childhood's matin dew
Fix'd, ere exhaled, in the Soul's adamant!

Mary with these had part; to her help came—
That help the proud despise. One eve it chanced
Upon the vast and dusking quays she stood
Alone and weeping. She that morn had sent
Her latest hoardings to her grandmother,
And half was sorry she had naught retain'd:
The warm rain wet her hair: she heard within
The silver ringing of its drops commingling
With that still mere beside her childhood's home,
And with the tawny sedge that girt it round,
And with its winter dogwood far away
Reddening the faint, still gleam. As thus she stood
Upon her shoulder sank a hand. She turn'd:
It was a noble lady, clothed in black,
And veil'd. That veil thrown back, she recognized
At once the luminous stillness and the calm
Ethereal which the sacred cloister breeds.
A voice as pure and sweet as if from heaven
Toned, as friend speaks to friend, address'd her thus:
"You lack a home: our convent is hard by."
  The lady, Spanish half, and Irish half,
No answer sought; but with compulsion soft
Drew her, magnetic, as the tree hard by
Draws the poor creeper on the ground diffused,
And lifts it into light. The child's cold hand
Lurk'd soon in hers: and in that home which seem'd
An isle of heaven the meek lay-sister lived
(Ere long by healthier airs to strength restored)
A rapturous life of Christian freedom, mask'd
In what but servitude had been to one
Lacking vocation true. The Life Divine,

"Hidden with God," is hidden from the world,
Lest Virtue should be dimm'd by Virtue's praise.
Heroic Virtue least by men is prized:
The hero in the saint the crowd can honor,
The saint at best forgive. To this world's ken
Convents, of sanctity chief citadels,
(Though sanctity in every place is found,)
The snowy banners and bright oriflambs
Of that resplendent realm by Counsels ruled,
Not Precept only, spread in vain, despised,
Or for their earthly good alone revered,
Not for their claims celestial. Different far
The lesson Mary learn'd. The poor were fed,
The orphan nursed; around the sick man's couch
Gentle as light hover'd the healing hand;
And beautiful seem'd, on mountain-tops of truth,
The foot that brought good tidings! Times of trial
Were changed to Sabbaths; and the rude, rough girl,
Waiting another service, found a home
Where that which years had marr'd return'd once more
Like infant flesh clothing the leprous limb.
Yet these things Mary found were blossoms only:
The tree's deep root was secret. From the Vow
Which bound the Will's infinitude to God,
Upwell'd that peaceful strength whose fount was God:
From Him behind His sacramental veil
In holy passion for long hours adored,
Came that great Love which made the bonds of earth
Needless, thence irksome. Wondering, there she learn'd
The creature was not for the creature made,
But for the sole Creator; that His kingdom,

Glorious hereafter, lies around us here,
Its visible splendor painfully suppressing,
And waiting its transfigurance. Was it strange,
If while those Brides of Christ around her moved
Her heart sang hymns to God? Much had she suffer'd:
Much of her suffering gladly there she learn'd
Came of her fault; and much had kindliest ends
Not yet in her fulfill'd. A light o'ershone her
Which slays Illusion, that white snake which slimes
The labyrinth of self-love's more tender ways—
Virtue's most specious mimic. She was loosed:
The actual by the seeming thraldom slain;
Her life was from within and from above;
And as, when Winter dies, and Spring new-born
Her whisper breathes o'er earth, the earlier flowers
(Unlike the wine-dark growths of Autumn, dipped
In the year's sunset) rise in lightest hues,
An astral gleam, white, green, or delicate yellow,
More light than color, so the maiden's thoughts
Flash'd with a radiance that permitted scarce
Human affections tragic. Oft, she told me,
As faithless to old friends she blamed herself:—
One hand touched Calvary, one the Eternal Gates;
The present nothing seem'd. The years pass'd on:
The honeymoon of this heart-bridal waned;
But nothing of its spousal truth was lost,
Nor of its serious joy. If failures came—
And much she marvell'd at her slow advance,
And for the first time (pierced by that stern grace
Wherein no sin looks trivial) fear'd;—what then?
Failures that deepen'd humbleness but sank

Foundations deeper for a loftier pile
Of solid virtue: transports homeward summon'd
For more disinterested love made way,
More perfect made Obedience.
If a Soul,
Half-way to heaven, death past, once more to earth
Were sent, it could but feel as Mary felt
When on the convent grates a letter smote
Loud, harsh, with summons from the outward world.
Her sister, such its tidings, was a wife,
(That matron whom you praised:—ay, comely is she,
And good; laborious, kindly, faithful, true;
Yet Time has done Time's work, her spiritual beauty
Transposing gently to a lower key;)
Her grandmother bereft, and weak through age,
Needed her tendance sorely. Would she come?
Alas! what could she? Duty stretched from far
An iron hand that stay'd her mounting steps;
The little novices wept loud, "Abide!"
Long on her neck the saintly sisterhood
Hung ere they bless'd her: then she turn'd and went.

And so once more she trod this rocky vale,
And scarcely older look'd at twenty-six
Than at sixteen. Before so gentle, now
A humbler gentleness was o'er her thrown;
Nor ruffled was she ever as of yore
With gusts of flying spleen: nor fear'd she now
Hindrance unlovely, or the word that jarr'd.
The sadness hers at first dispers'd ere long,
And such strange sweetness came to her, men said
A mad dog would not bite her. Lowliest toils

Were by her hand ennobled: Labor's staff
Beneath it burst in blossom. In the garden,
'Mid earliest birds, and singing like a bird,
She moved, her grandmother asleep. She mix'd
The reverence due to years with tenderness
The infant's claim. 'Twas hers the crutch to bring,
Nor mark the lameness; hers with question apt
To prompt, not task, the memory. Tales twice-told
Wearied not her, nor orders each with each
At odds, nor causeless blame. Wiles she had many
To anticipate harsh moods, lest one rash word
Might draw a cloud 'twixt helpless eld and heaven,
Blotting the Eternal Vision felt, not seen,
By hearts in grace. With works of gay caprice,
Needless—yet prized—she made the spectre Want
Seem farther off. Thus love in narrow space
Built a great world. The grandmother preferr'd
To her, that dreamful girl of old, the woman
Who from the mystic precinct first had learn'd
Humanity, yet seem'd a human creature
By some angelic guest o'er-ruled. At heart
Ever a nun, she minister'd with looks
That heal'd the sick. The newly-widow'd door
Its gloom remitted when she pass'd; stern foes
Down trod their legend of old wrongs. To her
Sacred were those that grieved; — those tearless yet
Sacred scarce less because they smiled, nor knew
The ambush'd fate before them. When a child,
Grey-hair'd companionship or solitude
Had pleased her more than childish ways; but now
All the long eves of summer in the porch

The children of her sister and the neighbors,
A spotless flock, sat round her. From her smiles
The sluggish mind caught light, the timid heart
Courage and strength. Unconscious thus, each day
Her soft and blithesome feet one letter traced
In God's great Book above. So pass'd her life ;—
Sorrow had o'er it hung a gentle cloud ;
But, like an autumn-mocking day in Spring,
Dewy and dim, yet ending in pure gold,
The sweets were sweeter for the rain, the growth
Stronger for shadow.
                    You have seen her tomb !
Upon the young and beautiful it closed :
Her grandmother yet lingers ! What is Time ?
Shut out the sun, and all the summer long
The fruit-tree stands as barren as the rock ;
May's offering March can bring us. Of the twain
The younger doubtless in the eyes of God
Had inly lived the longest. She had learn'd
From action much, from suffering more, far more,
For stern Experience is a sword whose point
Makes way for Truth. Her trials, great and little,
And trials ever keep proportion just
With high vocations, and the spirit's growth,
Had done their work till all her inner being
Freed from asperities, in the light of God
Shone like the feet of some old crucifix
Kiss'd into smoothness. Here I fain would end,
Leaving her harbor'd ; but her stern, kind fates
Not thus forewent her. Like her life her death,
Not negative or neutral ; great in pains,
In consolations greater. Many a week

Much ail'd her; what the cause remain'd in doubt;
When certainty had come she trembled not.
Fix'd was her heart. Those pangs that shook her frame,
Like tempests roaring round a mountain church,
Shook not that peace within her! She was thankful;
"More pain if such Thy Will, and patience more,
This was her prayer; or wiping from moist eyes
The trembling tear, she whisper'd, "Give me, Lord,
On earth Thy cleansing fire that I may see
Sooner Thy Face, death past!"
Alleviations,
Many and great, God granted her. Once more
Her sister was her sister! Unlike fortunes
Had placed at angles those two lives that once
Lay side by side; and love that could not die
Had seem'd to sleep. It woke; and, as from mist,
Once more shone out their childhood! Laugh'd and flash'd
Once more the garden-beds whose bright accost
Had cheered them for their parents mourning. Tears
Remember'd stay'd the course of later tears;
The prosperous from the unprosperous sister sought
Heart-peace; nor wealth nor care could part them more;
And sometimes Margaret's children seem'd to her
As children of another! Greetings sweet
Cheer'd her from distant regions. Once it chanced
The nuns a relic sent her ne'er before
Seen in our vales, a fragment of that Cross
Whereon the world's Redeemer hung three hours:—

The neighbors entering knelt and wept, and smote
Their breasts; her hands she raised in prayer; and
straight
Such Love, such Reverence in her heart there rose
Her anguish, like a fiend exorcised, fled;
And for an hour at peace she lay as one
Imparadised. A solace too was hers
Known but to babes. Her body, not her mind,
Was rack'd; the pang to come she little fear'd,
Nor lengthen'd out morose the pang foregone:
Once o'er, to sleep she sank in thankful prayer.
A week ere Mary died all suffering left her;
And from the realms of glory beams, as though
Further restraint they brook'd not, fell on her
Yet militant below, as there she lay
In monumental whiteness, spirit-lit.
The anthems of her convent charm'd once more
Her dreams; and scents from woods where she had
sat
In tears. Then spake she of her wandering days;—
Herself she scarcely seem'd to see in them;
Plainly thus much I saw: When all went well,
Danger stood nigh; but soon as sorrow came,
Within that darkness nearer by her side
Walk'd her good Angel. In that latest week
Some treasures hidden ever near her heart
She show'd me: faded flowers; her mother's hair;
Gold pieces that have raised our chapel's Cross;
A riband by her youthful comrade worn:—
Upon its cover some few words I found
There traced when first beyond the western main

She heard the homeless cuckoo's cry well-known :
"When will my People to their land return?"
From the first hour her grandchild sank, once more
She that for years bed-ridden lay, had risen,
And, autumn past, put forth a wintry strength,
Ministering. Her frame was stronger than her mind ;
O'er that at times a dimness hung, like cloud
That creeps from pine to pine. Inly she miss'd
Her wonted place of homage lost ; she mused
Sadly upon the solitary future ;
But in her there abode a rock-like will,
And from her tearless service night or day
No man might push her. Seldom spake the woman :
She call'd her grandchild by her daughter's name,
(Her daughter buried thirty years and more,)
And once she said in wrath, "Why toil they thus?
Nora is dead." She labor'd till the end :
It came—that mortal close ! 'Twas Christmas Eve ;
Far, far away were heard the city bells :
The sufferer slept. At midnight I went forth ;
Along the ice-film'd road a dull gleam lay,
And a sepulchral wind in woods far off
Sang dirges deep. Upon her crutches bent
The aged woman stood beside the door,
With that long gaze intense which is an act
Silently looking toward that hill of graves
We trod to-day ; a sinking moon shone o'er it—
Then whisper'd she—the light of buried years
Edging once more her eyes—"Each Saturday,
Of those that in that churchyard sleep three Souls,
Their penance done, ascend, and are with God."

Thus as she spake a cry was heard within,
And many voices raised the Litany
For a departing Soul. Long time—too long—
Had seem'd that dying ! Now the hour was come,
And change ineffable announced that Death
At last was standing on the floor. O hour !
When in brief space our life is lived again !
Down cast the latest stake ! when fiends ascend,
Beckoning the phantoms of forgotten sins
Conscience to scare, or launching as from slings
Temptations new ; while Angels hold before us
The Cross unshaken as the sun in heaven,
And whisper, "Christ." O hour ! when prayer is
all ;
And they that clasp the hand are thrown apart
By the world's breadth from that they love ! The
act
Sin's dread bequest, that makes an end of sinning,
Long lasted, while the heart-strings snapt, and all
The elements of the wondrous sensuous world
Slid from the fading sense, and those poor fingers,
As the loose precipice of life down crumbled,
Pluck'd as at roots. Storm-wing'd the hours rush'd
by ;
There lay she like some bark on midnight seas,
Now toiling through the windless vale, anon
Hurled on and up to meet the implacable blast
Upon the rolling ridge, when not a foot
Can tread the decks, and all the sobbing planks
Tremble o'erspent. The morning dawned at last,
Whitening the frosty pane ; the lights removed,
(Save that tall candle in her hand sustained

By others,) she descried it : "Ah !" she said,
"Thank God ! another day !" Then, noting one
Who near her knelt, she said, "The night is sped,
And you have had no sleep ; alas ! I thought
Ere midnight I should die." Her eyelids closed ;
Into a sleep as quiet as a babe's
Gradual she sank ; and while the ascending sun
Shot 'gainst the western hill his earliest beam,
In sleep, without a sigh, her spirit pass'd.
I would you could have seen her face in death !
I would you could have heard that last dread rite,
The mighty Mother's, o'er the stormy gulf
And all the moanings of the unknown abyss
Flinging victorious anthems, or the strength
Of piercing prayer : "Oh ! ye at least, my friends.
Have pity on me ! plead for me with God !"
That Rite complete, the dark procession wound
Interminably through the fields and farms,
While wailing like a midnight wind, the *keen*
Expired o'er moor and heath. At eve we reach'd
The graveyard ; slowly, as to-day, the sun
Behind a tomb-like bank of leaden cloud
Dropt while the coffin sank, and died away
The latest Miserere——
More than once
I would have ceased ; but he, my friend and guest,
Or touch'd or courteous, will'd me to proceed.
Perhaps that tale the wild scene harmonized
By sympathy occult ; perhaps it touch'd him,
Contrasting with his recent life—with England,
With Oxford, long his home ; its order'd pomp ;
Its intermingled groves, and fields, and spires,

Its bridges spanning waters calm and clear ;
The frequentation of its courts ; its chimes ;
Its sunset towers, and strangely youthful gardens
That breathe the ardors of the budding year
On the hoar breadth of grove-like cloisters old,
Chapels, and libraries, and statued halls,
England's still saintly City ! Time has there
A stone tradition built like that all round
Woven by the inviolate hedges, where the bird
Her nest has made and warbled to her young,
May after May secure, since the third Edward
Held his last tournament, and Chaucer sang
To Blanche and to Philippa lays of love—
Not like Iernian records. Sad we rose,
That tale complete ; and after silence, long,
As homeward through the braided forest-skirt
We trod the moonlight-spotted rocks, my friend
Resumed, with pregnant matter oft more just
In thought than application ; but his voice
Was softer than it used to be. At last,
After our home attain'd, we turn'd, and lo !
With festal fires the hills were lit ! Thine eve,
Saint John, had come once more ; and for thy sake,
As though but yesterday thy crown were won,
Amid their ruinous realm uncomforted
The Irish people triumph'd. Gloomy lay
The intermediate space ; thence brightlier burn'd
The circling fires beyond it. "Lo !" said I,
"Man's life as view'd by Ireland's sons ; a vale
With many a pitfall throng'd, and shade, and briar,
Yet overblown by angel-haunted airs,
And by the Light Eternal girdled round."

Brief supper passed, within the porch we sat
As fire by fire burn'd low. We spake ; were mute ;
Resumed ; but our discourse was gently toned,
(Touched by a spirit from that wind-beaten grave,
Which breathed among its pauses,) as of old
That converse Bede records, when by the sea,
'Twixt Tyne and Wear, facing toward Lindisfarne,
Saxon Ceolfrid and his Irish guest,
Evangelist from old Iona's isle,
'Mid the half Pagan land in cloisters dim
Discuss'd the Tonsure, and the Paschal time,
Sole themes whereon, in sacred doctrine one,
They differ'd ; but discuss'd them in such sort
That mutual reverence deeper grew. We heard
The bridgeless brook that sang far off, and sang
Alone : for not among us builds that bird
Which changes light to music, haply ill-pleased
That Ireland bears not yet, in song's domain
To Spenser worthy fruit. Our beds at last,
Wearied, yet glad, we sought. Ere long the wind,
Gathering its manifold voices and the might
Of all its wills in valleys far, and roll'd
From wood to wood o'er ridge and ravine, woke
A hundred peaks to me by sound well known,
That stood dark cluster'd in the night, and hung
With rainy skirt o'er lake and prone morass,
Or by sea-bays lean'd out procumbent brows,
Waiting the rising sun.

At morn we met
Once more, my friend and I. The evening's glow
Had from his feelings pass'd : in their old channels

They flow'd, scarce tinged. But still his thoughts retain'd
The trace of late impressions quaintly link'd
With kindred thought-notes earlier. Half his mind
Scholastic was; his fancy deep; the age
Alone had stamp'd him modern. Much he spake
Of England wise and wealthy—now no more,
He said, "a haughty nation proud in arms,"
Nor, as in Saxon times, a crownèd child
Propp'd 'gainst the Church's knee; but ocean's Queen,
Spanning the world with golden zone twin-clasp'd
By Commerce and by Freedom! But no less
Of pride and suffering spake he, and that frown
Sun-press'd on brows once pure. Of Ireland next:—
"How strange a race, more apt to fly than walk;
Soaring yet slight; missing the good things round them,
Yet ever out of ashes raking gems;
In instincts loyal, yet respecting law
Far less than usage: changeful, yet unchanged!
Timid, yet enterprising: frank, yet secret:
Untruthful oft in speech, yet living truth,
And truth in things divine to life preferring:—
Scarce men;—yet possible angels!—'Isle of Saints!'
Such doubtless was your land—again it might be—
Strong, prosperous, manly never! ye are Greeks
In intellect, and Hebrews in the soul:—
The solid Roman heart, the corporate strength
Is England's dower!" "Unequally if so,"
I said, "in your esteem the Isles are match'd:—

They live in distant ages, alien climes;
Native they are to diverse elements:
Our swan walks awkwardly upon dry land;
Your boasted strength in spiritual needs so helps you
As armor helps the knight who swims a flood."
He laugh'd. "At least no siren streams for us,
Nor holy wells! We love 'the fat of the land,'
Meads such as Rubens painted! Strange our fates!
Our feast is still the feast of fox and stork,
The platter broad, and amphora long-neck'd;—
Ill sorted yoke-mates truly. Strength, meanwhile,
Lords it o'er weakness!" "Never yet," I answer'd,
"Was husband vassal to an intricate wife
But roar'd he ruled her;" ere his smile had ceased,
Continuing thus: —"Ay! strength o'er weakness rules!
Strength hath in this no choice. But what is Strength?
Two Strengths there are. Club-lifting Hercules,
A mountain'd mass of gnarl'd and knotted sinews,
How shows he near the intense, Phœbean Might
That, godlike, spurns the ostent of thews o'ergrown;
That sees far off the victory fix'd and sure,
And, without effort, wings the divine death
Like light, into the Python's heart?—My friend,
Justice is strength; union on justice built;—
Good-will is strength — kind words — silence — that truth
Which hurls no random charge. Your scribes long time

Blow on our island like a scythèd wind:
The good they see not, nor the cause of ill:
They tear the bandage from the wound half-heal'd:—
In not such onset weakness? Were it better,
Tell me, free-trader staunch, for sister Nations
To make exchange for aye of scorn for scorn,
Or blend the nobler powers and aims of each,
Diverse, and for that cause correlative,
True commerce, noblest, holiest, frankest, best,
And breed at last some destiny to God
Glorious, and kind to man?—The choice is yours.

Thus as we spake, the hall clock vast and old,
A waif from Spain's Armada, chimed eleven:
And from the stables drew a long-hair'd boy
Who led a horse as shaggy as a dog,
A splenetic child of thistles and hill blast,
Rock-ribb'd, and rich in craft of every race
From weasel to the beast that feigns to die.
Mounting—alas! that friends should ever part,—
My guest bade thus adieu:—"For good or ill
Our lands are link'd." And I rejoined, "For which?—
This shall you answer when, your pledge fulfill'd,
Before the swallow you return, and meet
The unblown Spring in our barbaric vale."

ODE TO THE DAFFODIL.

I.

O LOVE-STAR of the unbeloved March,
  When, cold and shrill,
Forth flows beneath a low, dim-lighted arch
  The wind that beats sharp crag and barren hill,
  And keeps unfilm'd the lately torpid rill!

II.

A week or e'er
Thou com'st, thy soul is round us everywhere;
  And many an auspice, many an omen,
  Whispers, scarce-noted, thou art coming.
Huge, cloud-like trees grow dense with sprays and buds,
  And cast a shapelier gloom o'er freshening grass,
And through the fringe of ragged woods
  More shrouded sunbeams pass.
Fresh shoots conceal the pollard's spike
  The driving rack outbraving;
The hedge swells large by ditch and dike;
And all the uncolor'd world is like
  A shadow-limn'd engraving.

III.

Herald and harbinger! with thee
Begins the year's great jubilee!

Of her solemnities sublime
(A sacristan whose gusty tape.
Flashes through earliest morning vapor)
Thou ring'st dark nocturns and dim prime.
Birds that have yet no heart for song
Gain strength with thee to twitter;
And, warm at last, where hollies throng,
The mirror'd sunbeams glitter.
With silk the osier plumes her tendrils thin:
Sweet blasts, though keen as sweet, the blue lake wrinkle;
And buds on leafless boughs begin
Against grey skies to twinkle.

IV.

To thee belongs
A pathos drown'd in later scents and songs!
Thou com'st when first the Spring
On Winter's verge encroaches;
When gifts that speed on wounded wing
Meet little save reproaches!
Thou com'st when blossoms blighted,
Retracted sweets, and ditty,
From suppliants oft deceived and spited
More anger draw than pity!
Thee the old shepherd, on the bleak hill-side,
Far distant eyeing leans upon his staff
Till from his cheek the wind-brush'd tear is dried:
In thee he spells his boyhood's epitaph.

To thee belongs the youngling of the flock,
  When first it lies, close-huddled from the cold,
Between the sheltering rock
  And gorse-bush slowly over-crept with gold.

V.

Thou laugh'st, bold outcast, bright as brave,
When the wood bellows, and the cave,
And leagues inland is heard the wave!
  Hating the dainty and the fine
  As sings the blackbird thou dost shine!
Thou com'st while yet on mountain lawns high up
  Lurks the last snow-wreath: — by the berried breer
While yet the black spring in its craggy cup
  No music makes or charms no listening ear.
Thou com'st while from the oak stock or red beech
Dead Autumn scoffs young Spring with splenetic speech;—
When in her vidual chastity the Year
With frozen memories of the sacred past
  Her doors and heart makes fast,
And loves no flower save those that deck the bier:—
      Ere yet the blossom'd sycamore
      With golden surf is curdled o'er;
      Ere yet the birch against the blue
      Her silken tissue weaves anew.
Thou com'st while, meteor-like 'mid fens, the weed
  Swims, wan in light; while sleet-showers whitening glare;—
Weeks ere by river-brims, new furr'd, the reed
  Leans its green javelin level in the air.

VI.

Child of the strong and strenuous East!
Now scatter'd wide o'er dusk hill bases,
Now mass'd in broad, illuminate spaces;—
Torch-bearer at a wedding feast
Whereof thou may'st not be partaker,
But mime, at most, and merry-maker;—
Phosphor of an ungrateful sun
That rises but to bid thy lamp begone:—
Farewell! I saw
Writ large on woods and lawns to-day that Law
Which back remands thy race and thee
To hero-haunted shades of dark Persephoné.
To-day the Spring has pledged her marriage vow:
Her voice, late tremulous, strong has grown and steady:
To-day the Spring is crown'd a queen: but thou
Thy winter hast already!
Take my song's blessing, and depart,
Type of true service—unrequited heart.

A TALE

OF THE MODERN TIME.

PART I.

I.

An old man once I knew whose aged hair
A summer brilliance evermore retained:
Youthful his voice and full, not flawed nor spare;
His cheek all smooth, and like a child's engrained

Or marble altar innocently stained
With roses mirrored in its tablet white—
Like May his eye: his foot-fall slow but light.

II.

Yet no one marvelled at him: of his ways
Rarely men spake, as of the buried dead;
And dropped him from their lips with trivial phrase.
"Gentle he was, and kind," the neighbors said,
"Albeit an idle life, and vain, he led."
Odors he loved from flowers at twilight dim;
And breath and song of morn: children loved him.

III.

I have beheld him on a wintry plant
An eye delighted bending full an hour,
As though the Spring o'er every tendril scant
Crept 'neath his ken! Methought he had the power
To see the growing root plain as the flower.
O'er a leaf's margin he would pore and gaze
As o'er some problem of the starry maze!

IV.

Over a rose his palm he loved to curve
As though it brought him warmth from out the ground:
Instinctively his step would often swerve
Following slow streams that down in darkness wound:

His body there he bent above the sound,
Heard but by him. Some virgin world he trod,
As though it were the vesture of a god.

V.

I wondered at him long: but youth and awe
Restrained me from demanding of his story.
At last, it chanced one day, this man I saw
Reclining 'neath an oak rifted and hoary,
Last tree of a wild, woodland promontory:
Far round, below, the forest deep and warm
Lay waving in the light of an illumined storm.

VI.

I placed me at his feet: his eyes were closed—
Celestial brightness hung upon his mien,
And all his features, tranquilly composed:
I gazed on him, and cried, "Where hast thou been
In youth? What done, what read, what heard, what seen?"
Irreverent was the inquest: yet the man
Looked on me with a smile, and thus began.

VII.

The Tale, true told, of every Human Being
Were awful—yet upon each new-born child,
As though none lived beside, the Eye All-seeing
Rested in glory! Heaven looked down and smiled:

And choirs of joyful Angels undefiled
Around the cradle sang, and evermore
In youth walked near him, after, and before.

VIII.

Stranger! the veil of Sense in mercy hides
The perils round us, as the mercies! Say,
Amid the forests—on the mountain sides—
What miles of mazes hast thou tracked to-day?
Had some black chasm girt visibly thy way,
Couldst thou secure have wandered thus? Not so—
The danger is not ours while danger none we know.

IX.

My life hath been a marvel: thine no less.
If thou that marvel hast not yet discerned,
Lament not therefore. Unto wretchedness
That Knowledge grew for which our parents yearned.
The best and happiest ofttime least have learned
Of Man's dread elements—what dust—what spirit—
That which we are, what have, what make, and what inherit.

X.

Action in trance, in panic Thought were lost,
If all we are we knew ourselves to be.
O'er a great deep, now calm, now tempest-tossed,
Rises one rock; but, hid below the sea,
That rock slants down—a mountain! Such are we—

Our being's summit only o'er the deeps
Ascends: the rest is blind, and in the abysses
sleeps.

XI.

In Man the Finite from the Depth ascends—
Centre is Man of all men hear or see;
Chapel where Time with Incorruption blends,
Where Dust is wedded to Divinity.
All but omnipotent in Will is he.
Freedom his awful privilege! Like a God
He walks at noon; at night lies cold beneath the
sod.

XII.

Thou seekest Knowledge: every lore we prize
But as a lamp thereby ourself to know.
Stranger! 'tis well within to turn our eyes.
If we look heavenward, having turned them so,
Horror unnamed, and phantom forms of woe
Rebuke the haughtier quest. With single aim
If thou my tale require, receive in joy the same.

PART II.

I.

HAPPY my childhood was; devout and glad:
My youth was full of glory, joy, and might,
Like some volcanic morn, and tempest-clad,
In tropic regions, when from gulfs of night
Day leaps at once to the empyreal height.

Strength without bound in spirit, body, and soul,
I felt: and in my rapture mocked control.

II.

In the madness of that strength, I went abroad
  Where'er Ambition called, or Passion led:
Full many a deep my ploughing bark hath scored:
  Full many a plain hath echoed to my tread:
  All enterprise I sought: all books I read:
All thoughts I pondered, murmuring in my mirth
That text, "Be thou, O Man, the Lord of Earth."

III.

Deeply I studied, in all tomes and tongues,
  The Historic Legend, Philosophic page:
More deeply yet those earlier mythic songs
  Built up by Bard for legislative Sage,
  Himself a builder up, from age to age,
Of States—true poems—Policies sublime,
Wherein well-balanced Functions metre make and
    rhyme.

IV.

All Art and Science at the Gentile feast
  Of Western pride advanced, I knew right well:
And laughed to mark the great Book of the East
  Push on through all, as through a garden dell
  Bright with pale flowers, and paved with glittering
    shell,
Some Asian Elephant. I sought within
For God, and there alone; and recked not of my sin.

V.

Corporeal instincts only I denied:
My larger concupiscence temperance feigned.
Humble oft seemed I through the excess of pride,
And calm of conscious strength. No muscle strained;
That which the eye desired, the hand attained.
Too proud for Pride's less triumphs, I had sworn
Such victories first to master,—then to scorn.

VI.

Was I then wicked? Child! applauding nations,
Such question asked, had called me great and good.
I loved my kind—but more their acclamations:
My thoughts were birds of prey, and snatched that food
From weak and strong to gorge their infant brood:—
Much knowing, this I knew not. But the hour
Was come that proved at last my fancied power.

VII.

One day a mountain's summit I was pacing:
Through cloudy chasms the sunbursts fell thereon;
Over its plains the mighty winds were racing,
Quiring Eolian anthems in loud tone.
Long time I walked in pride, and walked alone:
And what I was revolved—and turned again,
To mark the far off towns and visible main.

VIII.

Man I considered then: and I looked forth
  Upon the works and wonders of his hand;
The deep his beaten road, his palace earth;
  Commanding all things; yet beneath command
  Of Mind—whereof I grasped the magic wand.
—Fronting the sun, that set in blood, I saw
Man's Shape against its disk; and yet I felt not awe.

IX.

All treasures of my Thought again I spread
  Unrolled as in a map before my eyes;
And walked among them with a conqueror's tread,
  That moves o'er fields of hard-won victories,
  Dreaming of mightier yet. A long disguise
Fell from me in that rapture; and I trod
A worshipper no longer but a God!

X.

Towards me a throne descended through the air—
  When lo! the crown of my demoniac Pride
Updrawn, raised up my horror-stricken hair!
  For, wheresoe'er I wandered, by my side
  Another step appeared to tread and glide:
No mortal form was near: and in the abyss
Of heaven, the mountain floors are echoless.

XI.

I stopped ; it stopped : I walked ; it walked : I turned :
  My fears I mocked, unworthy of a man.
Then a cold poison from that heart self-spurned
  Welled forth : and I, with eyes unfilmed, began
  Once more my life and inmost heart to scan :
Till suddenly what shape in soul I was
Before me I beheld plainly as in a glass.

XII.

Then my disease I knew ; but not the cure :
  Lightning, sent flaming from the breast of heaven,
Revealed my sins long-hid, from lure to lure :
  Beams from the eyes of God, like shafts were driven
  Against me : to her depth my soul was riven,
Whereof each portion, conscious and amazed,
In stupor of despair upon the other gazed.

XIII.

Thus on my throne, that marble mountain height,
  My Soul I saw! I went I know not whither :
Down like a tempest fell from heaven the night :
  I heard the sea, and rushed in panic thither ;
  By ghost-like clouds, and woods my steps made
      wither,
And rock, and chasm that seemed to gape and sever,
I rushed—and rushed, methought, for ever and for
      ever.

PART III.

I.

I WOKE in a great cavern of the main:
The wave rolled in, upon its strong breast bearing
A storm of icy wind and cloudy rain,
With sound as if of souls that died despairing:
The billows, that rough beach harrowing and tearing,
Thundered far off: while morning, just begun,
Peered dimly through the spray, and through the shadows dun.

II.

That shore was piled with death, like Nature's bier.
There, whitening spread a sea-beast's mouldering bones:
The rifted wings of a dead eagle here:
Over the wet cliff went funereal moans:
Yet calm at first I paced those wave-washed stones,
Whose crash the deadlier sound awhile could quell
Of that low step close by, my spirit's knell.

III.

Still, still, where'er I turned that step would follow.
My fate above me hung as by a thread:
Beneath me yawned the earth, a vast veiled hollow!
To battle-fields, athirst for death I fled.
Yet there, while headlong hosts beside me sped,
That footstep still I heard and knew from all;
Now harsh, now dull as moth fretting a coffin's pall.

IV.

Thick, thick like leaves from autumn's skeleton woods
 The shafts went by me, and as idly went.
Then back I turned into my solitudes,
 As slow, in sullen cloud of rage o'er-spent,
 As mountain beast into dim forest tent,
With hunger unabated, when the night
Melts; and the eastern wolds spread wide in hated light.

V.

Stranger! I tell you part: I speak not all.
 Thenceforth I walked alone; and joined my kind
Only when lured by some black funeral:
 On capital cities oft, with watchings blind,
 I gazed, what time rushed forth the freezing wind
Between their turrets and the wintry stars;
All day I lay in tombs, or caves dim-lit with spars.

VI.

On peaks eclipsing to its rim the ocean
 Hath been my dwelling: rivers I have seen
Whose sound alone dispersed a gradual motion
 O'er cloud-like woods, their deep primeval screen.
 Sand-worlds my feet have trod beneath the sheen
Of spheres unnamed. From zone to zone I fled,
As though each land in turn grew fire below my tread.

VII.

But Heaven had ended now my time of sorrow
  When most I seemed in penal horror bound:
Dreamless one night I slept, and on the morrow
  Strange tears now first amid the dew I found
  Wherewith my heavy hair and cheeks were drowned.
And in my heart, fanned by that morning air,
There lay, as I walked on, my childhood's long-lost
      prayer.

VIII.

Wearied, I sat upon a sunny bank,
  Ridged o'er a plain yet white with virgin snows,
Though now each balmy noon, and midnight dank,
  Lightened the burden of the vernal rose;
  My eyes (their wont it was till daylight's close)
Fixed on my own still shadow—in that light
Intense—keenly defined, and dark as night.

IX.

I hung above it: sudden, by that shade
  Another Shadow rested; faint and dim:
At first I thought my tears the phantom made;
  Then cried, "I do but dream it, form and limb."
  In horror then abroad I seemed to swim:
Then my great agony grew calm and dumb;
For now I knew indeed my destined hour was come.

X.

My spirit's Foe was now the spoil to claim
  My heart's chill seemed his hand upon my heart—
O marvel! clearer while that Shade became,
  No mocking fiend, I saw, no lifted dart;
  But a dejected Mourner! down, apart,
His head declined: one hand in grief he pressed
Upon the heaving shadow of a sorrowing breast.

XI.

The other round my neck was thrown, so fair,
  So kind, so gentle, none thereon might gaze,
Nor feel that Love alone had placed it there!
  There dropped the cloud of my Self-haunted days.
  He who for years had tracked my wandering ways
Had followed me in love! O Virgin-born,
Thy Shadow was the light of my eternal morn!

XII.

Stranger! there came a joy to me that hour;
  Such joy, that never can it leave my soul.
All Heaven, condensed to one ambrosial flower,
  Fell on my bosom—Truth's inviolate whole!
  Obedience was the Way; Love was the Goal:
God, the true Universe, around me lay:
Systems and suns thenceforth were motes in that clear
ray!

XIII.

From that time saw I what 'tis Heaven to see,
  That God is God indeed, and good to Man:
Theist then first. Who Love's Reality
  Hath proved, forgets himself to probe and scan.
  Knowledge for him remits her ancient ban:
Back fly those demons, outwardly to sin
That lure the soul, or turn our inquest sad within!

XIV.

Then looked I up; and drank from Heaven that light
  Which makes the world within, and world around,
Alone intelligible, pure, and bright:
  My forehead then, but not by me, was crowned:
  Then my lost youth, no longer sought, was found:
My penance then complete; or turned to pain
So sweet, the enamored heart embraced it like a gain.

XV.

My kind, new-vested in the eternal glory
  Of God made Man, glorious to me became:
Thenceforth those crowns that shine in mortal story
  I deemed it grief to bear, madness to claim.
  To be a man seemed now man's loftiest aim.
True Rule seemed this—to wait on one the least
Of those who fight God's fight, or join His kingly feast.

XVI.

Then the Three Virtues bade me kneel and drink:
  Then the Twelve Gifts fell from the heavenly tree:
Then from the Portals Seven, and crystal brink,
  Dread Sacraments and sweet came down to me.
  Then saw I plain that Saintly Company,
Through whom, as Living Laws, that world which Sense
Conceals, is ruled of God, by Prayer's omnipotence.

XVII.

Thus in high trance, and the way unitive,
  I watched one year: which sabbath ended, God
Stirred up once more my nest, and bade me live,
  Active and suffering. So again I trod
  The temporal storm, and wrestled with the flood;
And labored long; and, by His grace, behold,
Two grains I brought, or three, to swell the hills of gold.

XVIII.

Lastly, my faculties of body and mind
  Decayed, through God's high will and boundless love;
And from the trunk whereon they grew declined,
  As leaves from trees, or plumes from moulting dove.
  Thenceforth, more blest, I soared no more, nor strove;
But sat me down, and wait the end, as waits,
Sun-warmed, a beggar by great palace gates.

XIX.

Stranger ! this tale of one man's life is over :
  No knowledge mine in youth have I unlearned ;
But I the sense was gifted to discover
  Of lore possessed long since, yet undiscerned :
  Truths which, as abstract or remote, I spurned
In youth, as real most my heart now prizes ;
And, what of old looked real, now as dream despises ;

XX.

Or but like dreams reveres. Hollow and vain
  To me the pageants of this world appear ;
Or truth but symboled to the truthful brain :
  The future world I find already here ;
  The unbeholden palpable and dear :
Firm as a staff to lean on ; or a rod
Of power miraculous, and sent by God.

XXI.

Stranger, farewell ! Far off a bell is tolling :
  A bridal or a funeral bell—whate'er
It chaunts, in harmony the tones are rolling.
  All bells alike summon mankind to prayer !
  Yea, and for me those twain one day shall pair
Their blended chimes to one. When I am dead,
Stain not with tears my grave—it is a bridal bed.

XXII.

He ceased. The inmost sense of that I heard
  I know not: yet, because the man was wise,
His legend I have written word for word.
  All things hold meaning—to unclouded eyes
  Where eagle never flew are auguries.
It may be then this weed some balm doth bear;
Some cure for sight long dim—some charm against despair.

SONG.

I.

THOUGH oft beguiled, my friend, before,
  Still, still permit me to beguile;
Denounce not harshly, but deplore
  My laugh, and it may end a smile:
To children more akin than you
  We women are—we give them birth—
If we are sometimes childish too,
  Be men, nor war with childish mirth!

II.

Once on my head your hand you laid;
  I shook it thence;—but 'twas an art
To hide from you how near it weighed
  On that which shook beneath—my heart.

Go not: be cold, be stern, be mute;
  Yet stay: lest I, who cannot choose
But tremble sometimes at thy suit,
  At last should tremble to refuse.

SONNET.

FLOWERS I would bring if flowers could make thee
    fairer,
And music, if the Muse were dear to thee;
(For loving these would make thee love the bearer.)
But sweetest songs forget their melody,
And loveliest flowers would but conceal the wearer:—
A rose I marked, and might have plucked; but she
Blushed as she bent, imploring me to spare her,
Nor spoil her beauty by such rivalry.
Alas! and with what gifts shall I pursue thee,
What offerings bring, what treasures lay before thee;
When earth with all her floral train doth woo thee,
And all old poets and old songs adore thee;
And Love to thee is nought—from passionate mood
Secured by joy's complacent plenitude!

THE FALL OF RORA.

(FRAGMENT OF A LYRICAL DRAMA.)

SCENE—Outside Rora.

Shepherds, Villagers, Arnold.

ARNOLD.

LET all the women hence, and with the children
Hide near yon chapel of old pines. The Marquis
Advances ;—
See that all depart at once.
No time remains for wailings or farewells :
No, Shepherds, nor for wrath : the hour is come !

The offering which we offer up this day
In steadfastness of spirit we must offer,
And not in any passion. (*To Gianavello.*)
Place our men,
As I have said, before their cottage homes.

GIANAVELLO.

A little further north—

ARNOLD. (*In a whisper.*)

What, know you not
The entrance of the valley now is lost ?
Would you deny them their high privilege
Of dying near their homes—almost in sight

Of those that loved them, parents, brothers, children—
Our battle times are o'er: the end hath come.

THE BROW OF THE HILL BEFORE RORA.

The Marquis of Pianessa and troops.

PIANESSA.

I thank thee, Heaven! henceforth the way is smooth:
No rocks, no pine-stems! O that drop by drop!
How it made mad the thirst with which I burn!
Henceforth we are as free as fire, and onward
Rush, swift along the tempest of our rage.
Pause here awhile. Give me a cup of wine.

OFFICER.

Quick, bring some wine.

PIANESSA.

See you that village yonder,
With sunshine on its roofs? It smiles, like one
Who boasts of some short-lived impunity!
Glittering it stands among its orchards, bowers,
And vines—look down—'tis Rora! ay, 'tis Rora!

(*Soldier brings wine.*)

Three hundred men, my best, from Burner's hill
Were chased, a bloody track to Villaro!
Fill up the cup—two hundred men were hurled
From Peyro's summit to the waves beneath.

Fill up the cup—fill high—four hundred men
Down Bosca's chasms were dashed from rock to
rock—

(*Pauses—Officer presents the wine.*)

I will not drink it! Wine no more, nor bread,
Shall pass these lips, nor sleep assuage my breast,
While stands in yonder village, roof or wall.—
See you those rebels where they crowd? Look on
them!
Give me the cup—this wine shall be their blood.
Thus, thus, I pour it forth upon the ground!

(*Pours the wine on the earth.*)

Ha, ha, ye thought not I could wait so long!
Say, are the horses breathed?

OFFICER.

All fresh.

PIANESSA.

Then on!

Caverned rocks in the mountains above Rora.—Chorus of Virgins and Wives—Old Men, Children.

A GIRL.

It thunders!

AN OLD MAN.

No, it is their meeting.

A WOMAN.

Ah!
Thus far, beyond the sight of this dread battle
To wait the issue in suspense, and hear

No sound, but those fierce shouts, and our hearts' beating!
Hurl down, O wind, yon rocks! their jagged pines
Leave half the vale exposed, yet hide the battle.

SECOND WOMAN.

A tenfold shout—now, now they meet. O heaven!

CHORUS.

Clouds above the dark vale streaming!
Onward rushing, swift and free!
Oh! that, as a mirror gleaming,
You might shew us all you see!
Glittering heralds you should be
Of a sun-bright victory!

FIRST SEMI-CHORUS.

Now the battle hosts are meeting—
Tangled now in mazy error;
Like whirlpools down a river fleeting—
I am blind with doubt and terror.
Better death, than doubt. O cease!
Be still, my heart, or burst. Peace, peace!

SECOND SEMI-CHORUS.

Darkness and storm before him driven,
Ascending ever high and higher,
Yon Eagle cleaves the clouded heaven—
Lo! now sun-smitten, like a pyre
He burns! auspicious omen! we
Behold our Fate and Fame in thee!

FIRST GIRL.

Have we judged well?

SECOND GIRL.

To give up all at once!
The thought is glorious—

WOMEN.

But the act! woe, woe!

FIRST SEMI-CHORUS.

I heard a voice: the clouds were fled;
All heaven hung vast and pure o'er head;
The mountain rock, and mountain sod,
Lay steadfast, as the Word of God!
I heard a voice: it spake to me,
Far murmuring, "One hath died for thee,
That thou shouldst live both just and free."

SECOND SEMI-CHORUS.

"For how," that deep voice murmured—"how
Shall man to God his forehead bow,
Unless he first that sign august
Lift up—God's Image—from the dust?
Or how expand a chain-worn breast
For Christ therein, an equal guest,
To find his temple and his rest?"

FIRST WOMAN.

Alas! and see you those poor children straying
Still on, by cavern, brake, and rifted pine?
They seek, but hope no more to find the maid.

(*Children pass through the caverns singing.*)

I.

We have sought her in her bower;
In the garden we have sought her:
In the forest, hour by hour,
We have sought the chieftain's daughter.
She that was to us so tender,
Answer now she gives us none:
She is gone we know not whither.
If we knew where she is gone,
We would gather flowers, and send her
Those she loved, the last to wither.
Agnes! our beloved! come,
To thy children and thy home!

II.

She was not like others, gay—
But the mirthful loved her sadness:
And the mourner oft would say,
None could yield so soft a gladness.
As a star, remote and lonely,
Piercing depths of midnight woods,
Makes the dark leaves dance in lightness;
So into dejected moods,

She, that mournful lady only,
    Shone with beams of heavenly brightness.
Agnes, O beloved! come
To thy children and thy home!

III.

O beloved Agnes! where,
  Where art thou so long delaying?
O'er what mountains bleak and bare
  Are thy tender feet a-straying?
They have told us thou art taken
  To some palace white like snow;
    And some think that thou art sleeping:
  This we know not; but we know,
Every morning when we waken,
    All our lids are wet with weeping.
O beloved Agnes! come
To thy children and thy home!

CHORUS.

Hark, hark the Storm! the voice not long
Outstrips the Presence: see you now,
Not leaves alone, but branch and bough!
They roof the glen, a rushing throng,
Fast borne in current fierce and strong!
The cliffs that wall the vale are shaking:
The forests to their heart are quaking!
Crouch in caves who will: but I
Exulting pace this platform high!

My panting soul, with joy o'er-awed,
I cast upon the Storm abroad:
And soon will hurl, inspired by Wrong,
Thereon my vengeance and my song!

WOMEN.

Is it the gasping of the Storm
That makes her wan cheek red and warm?
Lo! how she fixes now her eyes—

CHORUS.

Catching the quickening impulse from those
kindling skies!
See, see the Storm grows radiant now,
As radiant as a lifted brow
Too long abased! lo, fast and wide,
Avenging Forms the tempest ride;
And answer, round, above, and under,
With choruses of rapturous thunder!
Burst on the tyrant, Storm from God!
Hurl them like leaves from rock to rock!
Trample them down through clay and sod:
From dark to dark!—their banners mock
The purple and the blood-stained gold
Thy clouds have vengefully unrolled—

WOMEN.

She lifts her hands, and far away
Flings forth the ban!

CHORUS.

For Tyrants say
That men were shaped but to obey:
Dead spokes alone, to roll and reel,
Within their car's revolving wheel!
Let them take heed, for they have driven
In frenzy o'er the rocky plain,
Till earth's deep groans are heard in heaven,
And fire bursts from those wheels amain—
Not soon the stormy flames expire
When hearts contagious in their ire
Burst forth, like forests catching fire!

II.

Or else this madness preys upon their spirit—
That all good things to man's estate which fall
Come from their sacred prescience—they inherit
Wisdom divine to nurse this mundane ball!
Yea, they apportion times; with care dispensing
The seasons; when to sow, what days for reaping,
What space for food and labor, praying, sleeping;
With stellar beams our harvests influencing;
Forth of the heaven of high conceit diffusing
Sunshine and breeze amid our murmuring grain;
Showering the former and the latter rain—
Or else with groans their vacant hours amusing,
And sending forth a famine, to fulfil
On men of froward heart the counsels of their will!
Such airy dream to realize,
All rights, all instincts they despise;
On every hearth they plant a foot,

Importunate, impure, and brute:
Round every bed a serpent creeps:
They make along the venomed wall
The hundred-footed Whisper crawl—
But Vengeance in a moment leaps
Forth from the frowning caverns of her noontide sleeps!

FIRST WOMAN.

How her high passion teems with thoughts as high;
Like fire from the Earth's heart quickening the seeds
In some volcanic soul to stateliest growth!
Flushed is her cheek with crimson as she cow'rs
Beneath their umbrage!

CHORUS.

Ha! how well
That Chief made answer. At the door
The herald stood, and shook all o'er;
And spake: "These tumults thou shalt quell;
Or else, a deep oath I have sworn,
Thy wife, the children of thy joy,
With fire in vengeance to destroy."
Then made he answer, without scorn:
"Their flesh thou mayest consume; Time must:
But I commend their spirits
To God, in whom we trust."

WOMEN.

See, see that man! he's hurt—how goes the battle?

MESSENGER.

Thrice have they rushed upon us: thrice fled back:
They form for the last onset. Arnold sent me—
He prays you to remove.

WOMEN.

We will not stir!
Why should we move?

MESSENGER.

The fight is worse than doubtful:
Fresh troops are pouring on us—Christoval—
Mario—the rest—have burst into the valley
From every entrance. We are girt—surrounded—

CHORUS.

Fight to the death! The Chieftain: lives he yet?

MESSENGER.

He lives.

CHORUS.

And Gianavello?

MESSENGER.

He is well.

WOMEN.

Ah! tell us, tell us—no, no, tell us not—
Tell us not who hath fallen.

MESSENGER.

Alas! alas!

WOMEN.

Speak not! speak not! we will bind up thy wounds;—
Thou art too faint!

MESSENGER.

Alas, poor Marguerita!
When all departed, she would not depart—

WOMEN.

Ah—what of her?

MESSENGER.

A bullet pierced her heart:
Staggering into her husband's arms she fell,
Crying aloud, "'Tis nothing, love, 'tis nothing:
It is God's will: fight thou unto the last;"
And so expired.

WOMEN.

Take, take that maid away—
See, she has fallen upon the rock in swoon.

CHORUS.

Smooth song no more; an idle chime!
'Tis ours, 'tis ours, ere yet we die,
To hurl into the tide of Time
The bitter Book of Prophecy.

For ages we have fought this fight;
  For ages we have borne this wrong.
  How long, Holy and Just! how long,
Shall lawless might oppress the right?

No dreamy influence numbs my song!
Too long suspended it has hung
Like glaciers bending in their trance
From cliffs, some horned valley's wall—
One flash, from God one ireful glance,
To vengeful plagues hath changed them all:—
Down, headlong torrents ('tis your hour
Of triumph) on the Invading Power!

Woe, woe to Tyrants! Who are they?
  Whence come they? Whither are they sent?
Who gave them first their baleful sway
  O'er ocean, isle, and continent?
Wild beasts they are, ravening for aye;
Vultures that make the world their prey;
Pests, ambushed in the noontide day;
Ill stars of ruin and dismay!
Tempestuous winds that plague the ocean:
Hoar waves along some rock-strewn shore
That rush and race, with dire commotion
Raking those rocks in blind uproar!

FIRST WOMAN.

She sings aright: this music of her anger
Makes my blood leap like founts from the warm earth:
My chill is past.

SECOND WOMAN.

'Tis well. We shall die free!

CHORUS.

As though this Freedom they demand of us
Were ours, at will to keep or to bestow!
To them a boon profane, a gift of woe;
For us a loss fatal and blasphemous!
This Freedom—man's dread Birthright of the Soul—
It is not man's, nor under man's control:
From God it comes; His prophet here, and martyr;
Which when He gives to man, man's sword must guard:
No toy for sport; no merchandise for barter;
A duty, not a boast; the Spirit's awful ward!—
Dread, sullen stillness, what art thou portending?
Once more each word I mutter on mine ear
(Forward in anguish bending)
Drops resonant and clear—
The forest wrecks, each branch and bough,
O'er voiceless caves lie tranquil now:
No sound, except the wind's far wail,
Forth issuing through the portals of the vale,
Now low, now louder and more loud,
Under the bridge-like archway of yon low-hung cloud!

FIRST WOMAN.

O God, what light is that? See, see, it spreads!
The vale is all one flame—the clouds catch fire—
Our hearths, our homes! all lost—gone, gone, for ever!

SECOND WOMAN.

It wakes another tempest! From the gorges
And deep glens on all sides the winds come rushing,
And mate themselves unto that terrible flame,
As we shake hands fiercely with our despair!
Lo, once again that sound! that flame, behold it!
Once more it leaps off from its burning altar
Up, up, to heaven—

CHORUS.

To be our witness there!

MESSENGER.

Arnold is dead! He felt the wound was mortal.
Then stood he up from slaying of his foes,
And smiled, and gave this staff to me, and said:
"If there be yet one free spot left on Earth,
Let them plant there this staff—
And there, not on my grave, remember me!"

CHORUS.

Is Arnold dead?

MESSENGER.

Arnold is dead: and with him
The freedom of the mountain-land is dead.
I too am dying; take ye then this staff;
And if there be one free spot left on Earth,
Plant it upon that spot: and be ye sure
Forth from this root shall grow the goodliest tree
That ever spread a green dome under heaven.

(*Dies.*)

FIRST SEMI-CHORUS.

Boast not, haughty conqueror!
  Not from thee hath fallen this woe:
He, the Lord of Peace and War,
  He alone hath laid us low.
Boast not, haughty conqueror!
  Slay, but boast not—Woe! Woe! Woe!

SECOND SEMI-CHORUS.

From Heaven the curse was shaken,
  On this predestined head:
From thy hand the plague was taken;
  By a mightier vengeance sped.
Mine is the sorrow,
  Mine, and for ever;
Who can turn back again
  A mighty archer's arrow?
Who can assuage my pain?
Who can make calm my brain?
  Who can deliver?

CHORUS.

I.

But within me thoughts are rising,
Severer thoughts, and soul-sufficing:
Swift, like clouds in exhalation,
  Come they rushing: whilst a glory
Falls on locks this fiery Passion
  Turns from black to hoary!

Voices round me borne in clangor
  Sound the trump of things to be:
And heavenly flashes of wise anger
  Give my spirit light to see
  The great Future; and aright
  Judge this judgment of to-night.

II.

I trembled when the strife began—
  Praying, my clasped hands trembled,
  With ill-timed weakness ill dissembled:
But now beyond the strength of man,
  My strength has in a moment grown;
  And I no more my griefs deplore
    Than doth a shape of stone—
A marble Shape, storm-filled, and fair
With might resurgent from despair,
I walk triumphant o'er my woe:
For well I feel and well I know,
That God with me this wrong sustains,
And, in me swelling, bursts my chains!

III.

And dost thou make thy boast then of their lying
  All cold, upon the mountain and the plain,
    My Sons whom thou hast slain?
    And that nor tears nor sighing
    Can raise their heads again?

My Sons, not vainly have ye died,
For ye your Country glorified!
Each moment as in death ye bowed,
On high your martyred Souls ascended;
Yea, soaring in perpetual cloud,
This earth with heaven ye blended—
A living chain in death ye wove;
And rising, raised our world more near those worlds above!

IV.

They perish idly? they in vain?
When not a sparrow to the plain
Drops uncared for! Tyrant! they
Are radiant with eternal day!
And oft, unseen, on us they turn
Those looks that make us inly burn,
And swifter through our pulses flow
The bounding blood, their blood below!
How little cause have those for fear
Whose outward forms alone are here!
How nigh are they to Heaven, who there
Have stored their earliest, tenderest care!
Whate'er was ours of erring pride,
This agony hath sanctified.
Our destined flower thy blasts but tear
Its sacred seed o'er earth to bear!
O'er us the storm hath passed, and we
Are standing here immovably
Upon the platform of the Right;
And we are inwardly as bright

As those last drops which hang like fire
Close-clustered on the piny spire,
When setting suns their glories pour
On yellow vales perturbed no more;
While downward from the eagle's wing
One feather falls in tremulous ring,
And far away the wearied storms retire.

V.

I heard, prophetic in my dreams,
The roaring of tumultuous streams,
While downward, from their sources torn,
Came pines and rocks in ruin borne:
Then spake that Storm to me and said,
"Quake thou with awe, but not with dread:
For these are Thrones and Empires rolled
Down Time's broad torrents, as of old.
But thou those flowers remember well,
By foaming floods in peace that dwell;
For thus 'mid wrecks of fear and strife,
Rise up the joys of hourly life;
And all pure bonds and charities
Exhale their sweetness to the skies—
But woe to haughtier spirits! They,
At God's command, are swept away,
Into the gulfs that know not day."

VI.

And now my Song is sung. I go
Far up to fields of endless snow.

Alone till death I walk: unsoiled
By air the tyrants have defiled.
Over a cheek no longer pale
I drop henceforth a funeral veil,
And only dimmed and darkened see
The mountains I have looked on free.
Ye that below abide, unblest,
Paint now no more with flowers yon dells;
Nor speak in tone like that which swells,
Loud-echoed from the freeman's breast:
In sable garments walk, and spread
With cerements black your buried dead.
Farewell to all: I go alone;
And dedicate henceforth my days
To muse on God's high Will, and raise
My hands toward th' eternal Throne—
And I beneath the stars will thread
The dark beads of my rosaries;
And ofttimes earthward bow my head,
And listen ofttimes for the tread
Of some far herald, swiftly sent,
To crown with light a shape time-bent,
And dry a childless widow's eyes
With tidings grave of high content,
Wherein unheeded prophecies
Shall find their great accomplishment!

SONNETS.

"LE RECIT D'UNE SŒUR."

I.

WHENCE is the music? minstrel see we none;
Yet soft as waves that—surge succeeding surge—
Roll forward—now subside—anon emerge—
Upheaved in glory o'er a setting sun,
Those beatific harmonies sweep on!
O'er earth they sweep from Heaven's remotest verge,
Triumphant Hymeneal, Hymn, and Dirge
Blending in everlasting unison.
Whence is the music? Stranger! these were they
That, great in love, by Love unvanquished proved:
These were true lovers, for in God they loved:
With God, these Spirits rest in endless day,
Yet still for Love's behoof, on wings outspread
Float on o'er earth, betwixt the Angels and the Dead!

II.

ALEXANDRINE.

Between two graves, a sister's grave and one
Wherein the husband of her youth was laid,
In countenance half a Spirit, half a Nun,
She stood: a breeze that branch of jasmine swayed
In her slight hand upholden: "Peace!" she said:
A smile all gold to meet the sinking sun
Came forth: the pale, worn face transfigured shone
Sun-like beneath the sorrowing widow-braid.
She raised that branch away her tears to wipe—
"How happy seemed our life twelve years ago!
I weep him still, but gaily weep at last!
Like some sweet day-dream looks that earthly past:
Of genuine joy the pledge it was, the type:—
Now, now alone the joy itself I know!"

III.

A HAPPY DEATH.

"How many a dear unwedded maid there is
Who—childhood's rapture over—thus might pray:
'God, God alone, can be our endless bliss,
Yet human love might have its little May!
The troth, the trust, the ring, the bridal kiss—
Had this been mine, I would not bid it stay!
Had this been mine, a year, a month, a day,
Had this been mine, and I been worthy this!
In spotless Love, blessing, to have been blest;
To have felt Earth's Love pierced through by Love
divine;

Rest to have known in Love, and Love in Rest:
Then the brief feast, contented, to resign;
To leave loved pledges with the loved—and die!'
—Sister, my dream was such; and lo, my wish have I."

NATIONAL APOSTACY.

TRAMPLING a dark hill, a red sun athwart,
I saw a host that rent their clothes and hair,
And dashed their spread hands 'gainst that sunset glare,
And cried, "Go from us, God, since God thou art!
Utterly from our coasts and towns depart,
Court, camp, and senate-hall, and mountain bare:
Our pomp Thou troublest, and our feast dost scare,
And with Thy temples dost confuse our mart!
Depart Thou from our hearing and our seeing:
Depart Thou from the works and ways of men;
Their laws, their thoughts, the inmost of their being:
Black Nightmare, hence! that earth may breathe again."
"Can God depart?" I said. Then one replied,
Close by—"Not so: each Sin at heart is *Deicide*."

WINTER IN THE WOODS.

When first the Spring her glimmering chaplets wove
This way and that way 'mid the boughs high hung,
We watched the hourly work, while thrushes sung
A song that shook with joy their bowered alcove:
Summer ere long o'er-arched with green the grove,
And deepening shades to flower-sweet alleys clung:
And last—one dirge from many a golden tongue—
The chiding leaves with chiding Autumn strove.
These were but Nature's preludes. Last is first!
Winter, uplifting high both flail and fan,
With the great forests dealt as Death with man;
And therefore through their desolate roofs hath burst
This splendor veiled no more by earthly bars—
Infinite heaven, and the fire-breathing stars!

ST. CUTHBERT.

What Power from Lindisfarne, the Holy Isle,
Drave Cuthbert to an islet yet more lone?
What bound the Anchoret to a cell of stone
By rough seas girt, and kept him glad the while?
Monks fly the world: he fled the Convent pile,
The anthemed rites of matins, prime, and none:—
What light was that which from his spirit shone
And lit grey rocks with never-waning smile?
Love, mighty Love! Nor bridegroom yet, nor
bride

In converse tranced, or linked, remote, in thought,
Has known his rapture! Loving, yet with awe
Thy Face, Eternal Love, for aye he saw:
Therefore of that wild cave he wearied not:
And in great peace his soul was satisfied.

MONASTICISM.

THE Spirit hath its Passion as the Sense:
A spiritual ear there is, a spiritual eye,
A spiritual heart whose "fires of light" supply
To the earthly heart Love's true Intelligence:
And, answering these, beyond thy narrow fence,
O Nature, spreads, remotest yet most nigh,
That spiritual Universe of Deity
Wherein alone Creation lives, and whence.
Behold the things that *are!* 'Tis we, alas,
That shadow-charmed, and drowned in things that *seem*,
Live without life, and die without a sign:
Alone the life monastic spurns the dream,
Crying to all the ages as they pass
"The strongest of Man's loves is love Divine."

POLAND AND RUSSIA.

I.

When, fixed in righteous wrath, a Nation's eye
Torments some crowned Tormentor with just hate,
Nor threat, nor flattery may that gaze abate:
Unshriven the unatoning years go by:
For, as that starry Archer in the sky
Unbends not his bright bow, though early and late
The Syren sings, and folly weds with fate,
Even so that constellated Destiny
Which keeps fire-vigil in a night-black heaven
Upon the countenance of the doomed looks forth
Consentient with a Nation's gaze on earth:—
To the twinned Powers a single gaze is given:
The earthly Fate reveals the Fate on high—
A Brazen Serpent raised, that says not, "live," but "die!"

II.

The Strong One with the Weak One reasons thus:—
"Through sin of thine our eagle wings are clipt:
Through frost of thine our summer branch is nipt:
Thy wounds accuse: thy rags are mutinous:
The nations note thine aspect dolorous
As some starved shape that cowers in charnel crypt,
Or landscape in eclipse perpetual dipt,
And, ignorant, cavil, not at thee but us!"

Then answer makes that worn voice, stern and
slow :—
"Am I a dog the scourger's hand that licks,
And fattens? Blind reproof but spurns the pricks.
That which I am thou mad'st me! long ago
My face thou grav'dst to be a face of woe,
Fixed as the fixed face of a Crucifix."

GALATEA AND URANIA; OR, ART AND FAITH.

"DREAD Venerable Goddess, whom I fear,
Gaze not upon me from thy starry height!
I fear thy levelled shafts of ruthless light,
Thine unfamiliar radiance and severe:
Thy sceptre bends not! stern, defined, and clear
Thy Laws: thy face intolerantly bright:
Thine is the empire of the Ruled and Right:
Never hadst thou a part in smile or tear!—
I love the curving of the wind-arched billow;
The dying flute tone, sweeter for its dying:
To me less dear the Pine tree than the Willow,
The mountain than the shadows o'er it flying—
Thus Galatea sang, (whilst o'er the waters
Urania leant:) and cowered 'mid Ocean's foam-
white daughters!

DEATH.

God's creature, Death! thou art not God's compeer!
An Anarch sceptred in primordial night;
Immortal Life's eternal opposite:—
Nor art thou some new Portent sudden and drear
Blotting, like sea-born cloud, a noontide sphere:
Thou art but Adam's forfeit by the might
Of Calvary sunset-steeped, and changed to light;
To God man's access through the gates of Fear!
Penance thou art for them that penance need;
To souls detached a gentle ritual;
Time's game reiterate and with lightning speed
Played o'er; through life a desert Baptist's call.
Judgment and Death are woeful things, we know:
Yet Judgment without Death were tenfold woe!

KIRKSTALL ABBEY.

Roll on by tower and arch, Autumnal River;
And ere about thy dusk yet gleaming tide
The phantom of dead Day hath ceased to glide,
Whisper it to the reeds that round thee quiver:—
Yea, whisper to those ivy bowers that shiver
Hard by on gusty choir and cloister wide,
"My bubbles break: my weed-flowers seaward slide:
My freshness and my mission last for ever!"

Young Moon from leaden tomb of cloud that soarest,
And whitenest those hoar elm-trees, wrecks forlorn
Of olden Airedale's hermit-haunted forest,
Speak thus, "I died; and lo, I am reborn!"
Blind, patient Pile, sleep on in radiance! Truth
Dies not: and Faith, that died, shall rise in endless youth.

UNSPIRITUAL CIVILIZATION.

We have been piping, Lord; we have been singing!
Five hundred years have passed o'er lawn and lea
Marked by the blowing bud and falling tree,
While all the ways with melody were ringing:
In tented lists, high-stationed and flower-flinging
Beauty looked down on conquering chivalry;
Science made wise the nations; Laws made free;
Art, like an angel ever onward winging,
Brightened the world. But O great Lord and Father!
Have these, thy bounties, drawn to thee Man's race
That stood so far aloof? Have they not rather
His soul subjected? with a blind embrace
Gulfed it in sense? Prime blessings changed to curse
'Twixt God and man can set God's universe.

ON A RECENT VOLUME OF POEMS.*

HID in each cord there winds one central strand:
Hid in each breast a panting heart doth lie:
Hid in the lines that map the infant's hand
There lurks, men say, a life-long destiny:
Through the dropt leaf 'gainst wintry sunset scanned
Shines that fine net whose strong geometry
Sustained the nascent shape, and each new dye
Fed by Spring dews, by pensive Autumn fanned.
Hid in this Book what note we? One Decree
Writ by God's finger on a destined soul,
That stamped each thought an act, and leaving free
The spirit, shaped the life into a whole.
What was that great behest—that mastering vow?
England, when Christ hath conquered, answer thou!

PENITENCE.

A SORROW that for shame had hid her face,
Soared to Heaven's gate, and knelt in penance there
Beneath the dusk cloud of her own wet hair,
Weeping, as who would fain some deed erase
That blots in dread eclipse baptismal grace:
Like a felled tree with all its branches fair
She lay—her forehead on the ivory stair—
Low murmuring, "Just art Thou, but I am base."

* By Dr. Newman.

Then saw I in my spirit's unsealed ken
How Heaven's bright Hosts thrilled like the gems of morn
When May winds on the sacred, snowy thorn
The diamonds change to ruby. Magdalen
Arose, and kissed the Saviour's feet once more,
And to that suffering soul His peace and pardon bore.

BOCCACCIO AND CERTALDO.

THE world's blind pilgrims, tendering praise for blame,
Passing Certaldo, point, and smile, and stare,
And with Boccaccio's triumph din the air:—
Ah, but for him how high had soared thy fame,
Italian Song! False Pleasure is a flame
That brands the Muses' pleasaunce—burns it bare
As some volcanic Island's barren glare:
O Italy! exult not in thy shame!
'Twas here, 'twas here thy Song's immortal river
Lost its last sight of hoar Parnassus' head,
And swerved through flowery meads to sandy bar:
Its saintly mission here it spurned for ever:
It sighed to Laura, and with Tancred bled:
But caught no second gleam from Dante's star!

A NIGHT ON THE GENOESE RIVIERA.

FANNED by sweet airs the road along the cliff
Wound in the moonlight, glistening now, now dim;
So winds a silver snake in pale relief
Girdling a sacrificial beaker's brim:
Black rocks loomed forth in giant hieroglyph
O'er silken seas: amid their shadows grim
From lowly town dim-lit, or dancing skiff,
At times the song was borne, at times the hymn.
Star after star adown the blue vault sliding
Their bright hair washed successive in the wave,
Till morning, from her far purpureal cave
Issuing, and o'er the foamless billows gliding,
Leaped, as the bells rang out from tower and shrine,
Up from her sea-bath to the hills of pine.

WRITTEN ON A SPOT BY THE ROTHA, NEAR AMBLESIDE.

I WALKED in dream. Alone the bright Boy stood
Half imaged in the waters round his feet:
His line had just been cast into the flood,
Then first; his glance leaped forth the spoil to meet!
The gold-brown curls about him waved, and sweet
The blithesome smile of parted lips; the blood

Flushing the fresh cheek like a rose whose hood,
With night-dews glittering, airs of morning greet.
Ah me! Since that glad moment sixty years,
Snow-laden, on their wintry pinions frore
Have sailed beyond the limit of our spheres,
And like that fleeting pageant are no more.
That Boy my Father was! the autumnal day
He led me to that spot his hair was grey!

October 17, 1862.

COMMON LIFE.

ONWARD between two mountain warders lies
The field that man must till. Upon the right,
Church-thronged, with summit hid by its own height,
Swells the white range of the Theologies:
Upon the left the hills of Science rise
Lustrous but cold: nor flower is there, nor blight:
Between those ranges twain through shade and light
Winds the low vale wherein the meek and wise
Repose. The knowledge that excludes not doubt
Is there; the arts that beautify man's life:
There rings the choral psalm, the civic shout,
The genial revel, and the manly strife:
There by the bridal rose the cypress waves:
And there the all-blest sunshine softest falls on graves.

MODERN DESPONDENCY.

WRITTEN IN DEVONSHIRE.

SOFT land, and gracious as some nectarous fruit
In whose warm bosom Autumn's heart is glad,
Thou hadst of old thy Bards,* whose lyre and lute
Well praised thy meads and woodlands blossom-
clad :
Thou hadst thy blithesome days ! If ours be sad,
May thy blue bays and orchards never mute
That sadness charm—slay causeless sorrow's root—
Loveless Self-Will, the Pride that maketh mad !
Wed, blameless Nature, wed with Grace Divine
Once more, like sweet harps blent with sweeter
voices,
Thy powers :—then sing, till child and man rejoices
Betwixt those "Double Seas" of England ! Shine,
Sun of past years ! Disperse those modern glooms
At least from golden Devon's Tors and Combes !

INDUSTRY.

VIRTUE defamed for sordid, rough, and coarse,
Unworthy of the glimpses of the moon,
Praise of the clown alone whose heavy shoon
Kneads the moist clay, nor spares the pure stream's
source,

* Herrick, William Brown, and others.

In thee how strong is grace! how fair is force!
How generous art thou, and to man how boon!
Not thine the boastful plain with carnage strewn,
Nor chambers wassail-shamed where late Remorse
Sits, the last guest! From ocean on to ocean,
From citied shore to hills far-forested,
The increase of earth is thine, in rest or motion;
The crown is thine on every Sage's head;
The ship, the scythe, the rainbow among flowers—
Thine too the song of girls exulting 'mid their bowers.

TO COLERIDGE.

WRITTEN IN EARLY YOUTH.

As one who lies, when day is almost done,
Rocked in a little boat upon a sea
Whose glassy billows heave eternally
Albeit the winds are lulled, watching the sun
That sinks behind those billows, and anon
Uprises, while the orange gleams that dye
The minster windows of the western sky
Are imaged in the waters smooth and wan;
Coleridge! thus hang we on the mystic traces
Of that one Thought which feeds thy soul with light;
Thus falls the "Idea of the Infinite"
Upon our dazzled lids and luminous faces;
Thus sinks, and reappears, and mocks our sight,
Absorbed once more in the great deep's embraces.

PONTEFRACT CASTLE.

WIND-WASTED castle without crown of towers!
Dread dungeon keep, watching the dying day!
A crownless king, great Edward's grandson,* lay
Wasting in thee, and counting prisoned hours!
A century passed: The Faith's embattled Powers
Thus far advanced; here stood, a stag at bay:
The eighth Henry trembled in his blood-stained bowers;—
Thou saw'st that "Pilgrimage of Grace" decay!
Two Woes thou saw'st—the fall of England's Crown,
That drowned in blood her old Nobility;
Then, baser plague, the old Temples trampled down
By Despots new! Twice-doomed! the fount in thee
I mark of that Red Sea which rolls between
England that is, and England that hath been!

TO THE MOST FAIR.

FAIR, noble, young! Of thee I thought to sing,
(If so Love willed, and the ever-virgin Muse
Who cannot grace accord unless Love choose,
Were pleased from Love's first bath, the Thespian Spring
One flower, or sparkling drop, on me to fling,)
For ofttimes thus some clan barbaric strews

* Richard II.

Its earth and wood, the little island's dues,
Before his feet whom conquest made its King :—
So dreamed I, when, a mourner sad and stern,
The Muses' Mother fixed on me her eyes—
Memory—nor slow their meaning to discern
Like a child stung I dropped the forfeit prize.
Some holier hand from out the immortal river
The destined reed must draw, and hymn thy praise
for ever !

FROM PETRARCH.

THAT nightingale which wails with such sweet woe
Haply its young ones, haply its dear mate,
Fills the dark heavens, and makes the fields overflow
With its wild, broken chaunt disconsolate :
Beside me all night long, where'er I go,
Its dirge reminds me of my own sad fate,
And chides my blindness which refused to know
That Death divine things too can subjugate.
Ah ! easy 'tis to cheat the self-deluded !
Yet who had ever dreamed those sunlike eyes
Setting, should leave the world in darkness shrouded ?
But I my pain's high mission recognize—
It means that I should weep and live, and so
Learn that delight abides not here below !

FROM PETRARCH.

Ah me! how beauteous were those tears of hers
The gathered cloud of Passion, melting, bred
When that deep grief whereon her heart had fed
Rose to her eyes, those tender, starlike spheres!
Wandered adown her delicate face her tears,
Wandered o'er pale cheeks touched with faintest
red,
As some clear stream through meads with flowers
o'erspread
(White flowers with sanguine mingled) softly steers.
Love in that rain bewitching stood embowered
Like blithesome bird on whom the longed-for rays
Blended with drops of gentlest rain are showered,
And, weeping 'mid his home in those fair eyes,
Shot from the bosom of that sad, sweet haze
Gleams of an ever-brightening Paradise!

A WARNING.

Why, if he loves you, Lady, doth he hide
His love! So humble is he that his heart
Exults not in some sense of new desert
With all thy grace and goodness at his side?
Ah, trust not thou the love that hath no pride,
The pride wherein compunction claims no part,
The callous calm no doubts confuse or thwart,

The untrembling hope, and joy unsanctified!
He of your beauty prates without remorse:
You dropped last night a lily; on the sod
He let it lie, and fade in nature's course:
He looks not on the ground your feet have trod:
He smiles but with the lips, your form in view;
And he will kiss one day your lips—not you.

PRINCIPLE A POWER; OR LOGIC IN HISTORY.

Lo! as an Eagle battling through a cloud
That from his neck all night the vapor flings,
And ploughs the dark, till downward from his wings
Fierce sunrise smites with light some shipwrecked
crowd
Beneath a blind sea-cavern beat and bowed;—
Thus through the storm of Men, the night of Things,
That Principle to which the issue clings
Makes fateful way, and spurns at last its shroud.
There were that saw it with a sceptic ken:
There were that saw it not through hate or pride:
But, conquering and to conquer, on it came,
No tool of man but making tools of men,
Till Nations shook beneath its advent wide,
And they that loosed the Portent rued the same.

COMPOSED AT RYDAL.

SEPTEMBER, 1868.

THE last great man by manlier times bequeath'd
To these our noisy and self-boasting days
In this green valley rested, trod these ways,
With deep calm breast this air inspiring breathed;
True bard, because true man, his brow he wreathed
With wild-flowers only, singing Nature's praise;
But Nature turn'd, and crown'd him with her bays,
And said, "Be thou *my* Laureate." Wisdom sheath'd
In song love-humble; contemplations high,
That built like larks their nests upon the ground;
Insight and vision; sympathies profound
That spann'd the total of humanity—
These were the gifts which God pour'd forth at large
On men through him; and he was faithful to his
    charge.

TO WORDSWORTH.

ON VISITING THE DUDDON.*

I.

So long as Duddon 'twixt his cloud-girt walls
Thridding the woody chambers of the hills
Warbles from vaulted grot and pebbled halls
Welcome or farewell to the meadow rills;
So long as linnets chant low madrigals
Near that brown nook the laborer whistling tills,

* See Wordsworth's "Sonnet to the Poet Dyer."

Or the late-reddening apple forms and falls
'Mid brakes whose heart the autumnal redbreast thrills,
So long, last Poet of the great old race,
Shall thy broad song through England's bosom roll,
A river singing anthems in its place,
And be to later England as a soul.
Glory to Him who made thee, and increase
To them that hear thy word, of love and peace!

II.

When first that precinct sacrosanct I trod,
Autumn was there, but Autumn just begun;
Fronting the portals of a sinking sun
The queen of quietude in vapor stood,
Her sceptre on the dimly-crimson'd wood
Resting in light. The year's great work was done;
Summer had vanish'd, and repinings none
Troubled the pulse of thoughtful gratitude.
Wordsworth! the autumn of our English song
Art thou:—'twas thine our vesper psalms to sing:
Chaucer sang matins;—sweet his note and strong;
His singing-robe the green, white garb of Spring:
Thou like the dying year art rightly stoled—
Pontific purple and dark harvest gold.

THE WORLD'S WORK.

WHERE is the brightness now that long
  Brimmed saddest hearts with happy tears?
It was not Time that wrought the wrong:
  Thy three-and-twenty vanquished years
Crouched reverent, round their spotless prize
  Like lions awed that spare a Saint;
Forbore that face—a paradise
  No touch autumnal ere could taint.

It was not sorrow. Prosperous love
  Her amplest streams for thee poured forth,
As when the Spring in some rich grove
  With blue-bells spreads a sky on earth.
Subverted Virtue! They the most
  Lament, that seldom deign to sigh;
O World! is this fair wreck thy boast?
  Is this thy triumph, Vanity?

What power is that which, being nought,
  Can unmake stateliest works of God?
What brainless thing can vanquish thought?
  What heartless, leave the heart a clod?
The radiance quench, yet add the glare?
  Dry up the flood;—make loud the shoal?
And, merciless in malice, spare
  That mask, a face without a soul?

Ah Parian brows that overshone
  Eyes bluer than Egean seas!
One time God's glory wrote thereon
  Goodwill's two Gospels, Love and Peace.
Ah smile! Around those lips of hers
  The lustre rippled and was still,
As when a gold leaf falling stirs
  A moment's tremor on the rill!

THE CHURCH'S WORK.

HER coral lip a sun-beam smote:
  Behind her shapely head
The white veil refluent seemed to float
  Like clouds in ether spread:
She looked so noble, sweet, and good,
  Love clapped his hands for glee,
And cried, "This, this is Womanhood—
  The rest but female be!"

So modest, yet confiding too—
  So tender to bestow
On each that loving honor due
  To all things, high or low,
Her soft self-reverence part had none
  In consciousness or pride,
A reflex of that worship won
  From her by all beside.

So creaturely in all her ways,
  So humbly great she seemed—
O Grecian lays, O Pagan praise,
  Of such ye never dreamed!
Through sunshine on she moved as one
  Innocuously possest
(Thy lot reversed, O Babylon!)
  By some angelic guest.

Buoyant as bird in leafy bower,
  As calm she looked as those
Who long have worn the nuptial flower
  Upon their matron brows:
Yet ten years hence, when girl and boy
  May mount her lap at will,
That virgin grace, that vestal joy
  Now hers will haunt her still!

A GIRL'S SONG.

UNKIND was he, the first who sang
  The spring-tide shamed, the flower's decay!
What woman yet without a pang
  Could hear of Beauty's fleeting May?
O Beauty! with me bide, and I
A maid will live, a maid will die.

Could I be always fair as now,
  And hear, as now, the Poets sing
"The long-lashed eyes, the virgin brow,
  The hand well worthy kiss and ring,"
Then, then some casual grace were all
That e'er from me on man should fall!

I sailed last night on Ina's stream:
  Warm 'mid the wave my fingers lay;
The cold-lipped Naiad in my dream
  Kissed them, and sighed, and slipped away—
Ah me! down life's descending tide
Best things, they say, the swiftliest glide.

A SONG OF AGE.

I.

WHO mourns? Flow on, delicious breeze!
  Who mourns, though youth and strength go by?
Fresh leaves invest the vernal trees,
  Fresh airs will drown my latest sigh.
What am I but a part outworn
  Of earth's great Whole that lifts more high
A tempest-freshened brow each morn
  To meet pure beams and azure sky?

II.

Thou world-renewing breath, sweep on,
  And waft earth's sweetness o'er the wave!
That earth will circle round the sun
  When God takes back the life He gave!
To each his turn! Even now I feel
  The feet of children press my grave,
And one deep whisper o'er it steal—
  "The Soul is His Who died to save."

STANZAS.

HER kiss, ere yet he snatched it thence
  On lips like rose-leaves twice had trembled:
The Bard, and Love's Intelligence
  Marked the brief trifle ill-dissembled:

Far off a horse's hoof we heard:
  She turned: her sunny blush we noted:
She sang as sings the enamored bird—
  That kiss within her fancy floated.

And just ere yet he reached the door,
  So shook that white vest ringlet-shaded,
Such sweetness sank those eyelids o'er,
  I knew that in her heart she made it!

Ah Girl! ah Child! To men a kiss
  Is oft a seal, dissolved or broken:
To Maids the seal impressed it is—
  Truth's solemn pledge—Joy's laughing token!

LINES.

Only a reed that sighed:—
  And the Poplar grove hard by
From a million of babbling mouths replied,
  "Who cares, who cares? Not I!"

Only a dove's low moan:—
  And the new-gorged raven near
Let fall from the red beak the last white bone,
  And answered, half croak, half sneer.

The pale, still face too soon
  Was paler, stiller thrice:
And ere the rose burst in the breast of June
  The young, warm heart was ice.

SAD MUSIC.

DESCEND into the depths forlorn
  Of this obscured and silent soul,
O Song! With gradual breath, like morn,
  Our spirits touch, and make them whole!

Blot thou base worlds, and make us see
  Those pitying Presences which stand
Round sensuous life perpetually,
  And beckon to the Spirit-land.

Teach us to feel the Truths we know:
  The shores we tend to—draw them nigh:
The things that leave us—bid them go
  With modulated movement by.

Song sad and sweet, the power be thine
  Breeze-like o'er life's suspended wreath
To sprinkle freshening dews benign,
  And waft us toward the gates of Death

With happier grace than his who reared
  The mild Caducean wand, and led
O'er Lethe's wave, no longer feared,
  The pensive Shades of Heroes dead.

LINES.

CAN a man sit mute by a fast-barred door
  While the night-showers cut through the shivering skin,
Yet love in her hardness, love on, love more,
  That cold-eyed Beauty who smiles within?
Such a man—he is dead long since—I knew:
There was one that never could know him—You!

Can a man from the gunwale his grasp relax
  Nor bend his brow, as he sinks in the tide,
At the veil held back by the hand of wax
  That might have saved him, yet help denied?
Such a man—he is dead at last—I knew:
There was one who never could know him—You!

My friend is dead:—it was time he died!
  His heart was yours while a pulse remained:
Red lips, do ye chide for pity or pride
  That the beaker ye quaffed so often is drained?
By that hand of wax, by that eye's cold blue,
The prize he lost was a loss for two!

MARCH OMENS.

On ivied stems and leafless sprays
  The sunshine lies in dream:
Scarcely yon mirrored willow sways
  Within the watery gleam.

In woods far off the dove is heard,
  And streams that feed the lake;
All else is hushed save one small bird
  That twitters in the brake.

Yet something works through earth and air,
  A sound less heard than felt,
Whispering of Nature's procreant care,
  While the last snow-flakes melt.

The year anon her rose will don;
  But to-day this trance is best—
This weaving of fibre and knitting of bone
  In Earth's maternal breast.

FEBRUARY.

WHAT dost thou, laggard Daffodil,
  Tarrying so long beneath the sod?
Hesper, thy mate, o'er yonder hill
  Looks down and strikes with silver rod
The pools that mirrored thee last year,
Yet cannot find thee far or near.

Pale Primrose! for a smile of thine
  Gladly to earth these hands would pour
An ivied urn of purple wine,
  Such as at Naxos Bacchus bore,
Watching with fixed black eyes the while
That pirate barque draw near his isle!

Shake down, dark Pine, thy scalp of snow—
  False witch, stripped bare, grim Ash-tree tall!
Ye ivy masses that now swing slow
  Now shudder in spasms on the garden wall,
Shake down your load and the borders strew;
The rosemary borders and banks of rue.

The Robin, winter's Nightingale,
  Hung mute to-day on the blackthorn brake:
We heard but the water-fowl pipe and wail
  Fluting aloud on the lake;
Who hears that bell-note so clear and free
Though inland he stands, beholds the sea.

As the moon that rises of saffron hue
  Ascending, changes to white,
So the year, with the Daffodil rising new,
  On Narcissus will soon alight :—
Rise up, thou Daffodil, rise ! With thee
The year begins, and the spring-tide glee !

WITH A BOOK OF VERSE.

He knew not, he that wrote this book,
  Thine eyes should one day glance thereon :—
So shines Aurora on a brook :
  Her splendor spreads ; the brook is gone.

Her glory dawns from height to height :
  He sinks through forest shades beneath :
Fate drags him down through caves of night
  Low-chaunting lessening songs of death.

Ah me, Aurora ! smile but thou
  On one poor page with beam benign !
No meaner radiance needs the brow,
  Or book, refreshed with light of thine !

APPEARANCES.

SCIENCE her sunless vigil kept
  In soundings of a league-deep sea:
The Hour had come: the Hour on swept
  From Time into Eternity.

Ambition o er the hills of War
  Tracked the red path which goal hath none,
Following its blind on-rushing star
  That circles round no central sun.

O'er palace fronts Imperial pride
  Raised the rich fretwork high and higher:
Through all its worlds, on wind and tide
  Trade rolled the wheels that never tire.

The Lover nursed his hectic dream;
  The Poet wailed a glory dead;
The Enthusiast chased a flying gleam,
  While, winged with Fate, the Hour on sped.

They sowed, they reaped, they woke, they slept:
  Free changed to bond, and bond to free:
Realm strove with realm, and sept with sept—
  These were the things that seemed to be.

That hour, unnoticed and unknown,
  An orphan laid him down to die:
That hour God reaped what God had sown:
  That was alone Reality.

DEATH.

FROM death the strongest spirit shrinks,
  For mystery veils the last dread strife:
None loves to die. And yet methinks
  We have been dying all our life.

When first thy childhood sang its hymn
  Above the opening bud, that hour
Thine Infancy with eyelids dim
  Lay cold in death, a faded flower!

When Youth in turn its place had won,
  What whispered Childhood's ebbing breath?
Sad words it sighed o'er bright things gone,
  And that First Sin, true Childhood's death.

And Youth was dead ere Manhood came:
  And Wisdom's fruits of bitter taste
Were rooted in a soil of shame,
  Poor funeral fruits of manhood's waste.

O Life, long-dying, wholly die,
  That Death not less may die at last:
And live, thou great Eternity
  That Present art at once and Past!

*ST. COLUMKILL'S FAREWELL TO THE ISLE OF ARRAN, ON SETTING SAIL FOR IONA.**

FROM THE GAELIC.

FAREWELL to Arran Isle,† farewell!
 I steer for Hy:‡ my heart is sore:—
The breakers burst, the billows swell
 'Twixt Arran Isle and Alba's § shore.

Thus spake the Son of God, "Depart!"—
 O Arran Isle, God's will be done!
By Angels thronged this hour thou art:
 I sit within my bark alone.

O Modan, well for thee the while!
 Fair falls thy lot, and well art thou!
Thy seat is set in Arran Isle:
 Eastward to Alba turns my prow.

O Arran, Sun of all the West!
 My heart is thine! As sweet to close
Our dying eyes in thee as rest
 Where Peter and where Paul repose!

* From the prose translation in vol. i. of the *Transactions of the Gaelic Society*, Dublin, 1808.

† In the Bay of Galway. It was one of the chief retreats of the Irish monks and missionaries, and still abounds in religious memorials.

‡ Iona.

§ Scotland.

O Arran, Sun of all the West!
  My heart in thee its grave hath found:
He walks in regions of the blest
  The man that hears thy church-bells sound!

O Arran blest, O Arran blest!
  Accursed the man that loves not thee!
The dead man cradled in thy breast—
  No demon scares him: well is he.

Each Sunday Gabriel from on high
  (For so did Christ our Lord ordain)
Thy Masses comes to sanctify,
  With fifty Angels in his train.

Each Monday Michael issues forth
  To bless anew each sacred fane:
Each Tuesday cometh Raphael
  To bless pure hearth and golden grain.

Each Wednesday cometh Uriel,
  Each Thursday Sariel, fresh from God;
Each Friday cometh Ramael
  To bless thy stones and bless thy sod.

Each Saturday comes Mary,
  Comes Babe on arm, 'mid heavenly hosts!
O Arran, near to heaven is he
  That hears God's Angels bless thy coasts!

CHARITY.

THOUGH all the world reject thee, yet will I
Fold thee, with all thine errors, in my heart,
And cherish even thy weakness! Who can say
That he is free from sin; or that to him
Belongs to speak the judgments of the Lord,
To vindicate the dignity of Heaven?
Behold the Master! prostrate at His feet,
Shuddering with penitential agony,
Magdalen! O those mild forgiving eyes,
Mercy and pity blossoming in Love!
O lips full founts of pardon and of blessing!
Shall I, a sinner, scorn a sinner, or
Less love my brother seeing he is weak?
Shall not my heart yearn to his helplessness
Like the fond mother's to her idiot boy?
O cruel mockery, to call that love
Which the world's frown can wither! Hypocrite!
False friend! Base selfish man! fearing to lift
Thy soiled fellow from the dust! From thee
The love of friends, the sympathy of kind
Recoil like broken waves from a bare cliff,—
Waves that from far seas come with noiseless step
Slow stealing to some lonely ocean isle;—
With what tumultuous joy and fearless trust
They fling themselves upon its blackened breast,
And wind their arms of foam around its feet,
Seeking a home; but finding none, return
With slow, sad ripple, and reproachful murmur.
No! No! True Charity scorns not the love
Even of the guiltiest, but treasures up

The precious gift within its heart of hearts,
Freely returning love where wanted most,
Like flowers that from the generous air imbibe
The essences of life, and give them forth
Again in odors. Spirit of Love Divine
That filled'st with tenderness the reverent eyes
Of Mary as she gazed upon her Babe,
Soften our stony nature; make us know
How much we need to be forgiven; build up
True Charity on humbleness of heart.

S. E. DE VERE.

ON VISITING A HAUNT OF COLERIDGE'S.

FROM Lynton, where the double streams
  Through forest-hung ravines made way,
  And bounded into seas late grey
That shook with morning's earliest beams,
  I wandered on to Porlock bay;

And thence, for love of him who sang
  His happiest songs beside their rills,
  To "seaward Quantock's heathy hills"
Advanced, while lane and hedge-grove rang,
  And all the song-birds "had their wills."

There, like a sweet face dimmed with pain,
  The scene grew dark with mist and shower:
  Its yellow leaf the autumnal bower
Moulted full fast; and as the rain
  Washed the last fragrance from the flower,

I heard the blue-robed schoolboy's tongue
  Thrilling Christ's Hospital once more
  With mystic chaunt and antique lore,
While round their Bard his playmates hung,
  Wondering, and sighed, the witchery o'er.

I saw him tread soft Devon's coombes :—
  Ah, thence he drew that southern grace
  Which in his song held happy place
Amid the shrouded northland glooms,
  Like some strange flower of alien race.

That Bard who like a gleam, or strain
  Of music, crossed at morn and eve
  Those hills, who sang of Genevieve,
And that weird Pilgrim from the main,
  Not less, at Truth's command, could leave

Song's sheltered haunt the heights to climb
  Where, passing cloud and precipice,
  Mind, throned among the seas of ice,
Watches from specular tower sublime
  Far visions kenned through freezing skies,

Outlines of Thought, like hills through mist
  That stretch athwart the Infinite
  In dread mathesis lines of light—
Such Thoughts the Muse's spell resist;
  Above her mark they wing their flight!

The songs he gave us, what were they
  But preludes to some loftier rhyme
  That would not leave the spheral chime,
The concords of eternal Day,
  And speak itself in words of Time?

O ever famished Heart! O hands
  That still "drew nectar in a sieve!"
  At birth of thine what witch had leave
To bind such strength in willow bands,
  The web half-woven to unweave?

Oh for those Orphic songs unheard
  That lived but in the singer's thought!
  Who sinned? Whose hand defeature wrought?
Unworthy was the world or Bard
  To clasp those Splendors all but caught?

What Bard of all who e'er have sung
  Since that lark sang when Eve had birth,
  Song's inmost soul had uttered forth
Like thee? from Song's asperge had flung
  Her lesser baptism o'er the earth?

The world's base Poets have not kept
  Song's vigil on her vestal height,
  Nor scorned false pride and foul delight,
Nor with the weepers rightly wept,
  Nor seen God's visions in the night!

Profane to enthrone the Sense, and add
  A gleam that lies to shapes that pass,
  Ah me! in song as in a glass
They might have shewn us glory-clad
  His Face Who ever is and was!

They might have shown us cloud and leaf
  Lit with the radiance uncreate;
  Love, throned o'er vanquished Lust and Hate;
Joy, gem-distilled through rocks of Grief;
  And Justice conquering Time and Fate!

But they immodest brows have crowned
  With violated bud and flower:—
  Courting the high Muse "par amour,"
Upon her suppliants she hath frowned,
  And sent them darkness for a dower.

Better half-sight and tear-dimmed day
  Than dust-defiled, o'er-sated Touch!
  Better the torn wing than the crutch!
Better who hide their gift than they
  Who give so basely and so much.

Thy song was pure: thy heart was high:
  Thy genius in its strength was chaste:
  And if that genius ran to waste,
Unblemished as its native sky
  O'er diamond rocks the river raced!

Great Bard! To thee in youth my heart
  Rushed as the maiden's to the boy,
  When love, too blithesome to be coy,
No want forebodes and feels no smart,
  A self-less love self-brimmed with joy!

Still sporting with those amaranth leaves
  That shape for others coronals,
  I ask not on whose head it falls
That crown the Fame Pandemian weaves—
  Thee, thee the Fame Uranian calls!

For wildered feet point thou the path
  Which mounts to where triumphant sit
  The Assumed of Earth, all human yet,
From sun-glare safe, and tempest's wrath,
  Who sing for love; nor those forget,

The Elders crowned that, singing, fling
  Their crowns upon the Temple floor;
  Those Elders ever young, though hoar,
Who count all praise an idle thing
  Save His who lives for evermore!

AUTUMNAL ODE.

DEDICATED TO MY SISTER.

OCTOBER, 1867.

I.

MINSTREL and Genius, to whose songs or sighs
The round earth modulates her changeful sphere,
That bend'st in shadow from yon western skies,
And lean'st, cloud-hid, along the woodlands sere,
Too deep thy notes—too pure—for mortal ear!
Yet Nature hears them: without aid of thine
How sad were her decline!
From thee she learns with just and soft gradation
Her dying hues in death to harmonize;
Through thee her obsequies
A glory wear that conquers desolation.
Through thee she singeth, "Faithless were the sighing
Breathed o'er a beauty only born to fleet:
A holy thing and precious is the dying
Of that whose life was innocent and sweet."
From many a dim retreat
Lodged on high-bosomed, echoing mountain lawn,
Or chiming convent 'mid dark vale withdrawn,
From cloudy shrine or rapt oracular seat
Voices of loftier worlds that saintly strain repeat.

II.

It is the Autumnal Epode of the year:
The nymphs that urge the seasons on their round,

They to whose green lap flies the startled deer
When bays the far off hound,
They that drag April by the rain-bright hair,
(Though sun-showers daze her and the rude winds scare)
O'er March's frosty bound,
They by whose warm and furtive hand unwound
The cestus falls from May's new-wedded breast—
Silent they stand beside dead Summer's bier,
With folded palms, and faces to the West,
And their loose tresses sweep the dewy ground.

III.

A sacred stillness hangs upon the air,
A sacred clearness. Distant shapes draw nigh:
Glistens yon Elm-grove, to its heart laid bare,
And all articulate in its symmetry,
With here and there a branch that from on high
Far flashes washed as in a watery gleam:
Beyond, the glossy lake lies calm—a beam
Upheaved, as if in sleep, from its slow central stream.

IV.

This quiet—is it Truth, or some fair mask?
Is pain no more? Shall Sleep be lord, not Death?
Shall sickness cease to afflict and overtask
The spent and laboring breath?

Is there 'mid all yon farms and fields, this day,
  No grey old head that drops? No darkening eye?
Spirits of Pity, lift your hands, and pray—
  Each hour, alas, men die!

V.

The love songs of the Blackbird now are done:
  Upon the o'ergrown, loose, red-berried cover
The latest of late warblers sings as one
  That trolls at random when the feast is over:
  From bush to bush the dusk-bright cobwebs hover,
    Silvering the dried-up rill's exhausted urn;
No breeze is fluting o'er the green morass:
Nor falls the thistle-down: in deep-drenched grass,
    Now blue, now red, the shifting dew-gems burn.

VI.

Mine ear thus torpid held, methinks mine eye
  Is armed the more with visionary power:
  As with a magnet's force each redd'ning bower
Compels me through the woodland pageantry:
Slowly I track the forest's skirt: emerging,
  Slowly I climb from pastoral steep to steep:
I see far mists from reedy valleys surging:
  I follow the procession of white sheep
  That fringe with wool old stock and ruined rath,
How staid to-day, how eager when the lambs
Went leaping round their dams!
I cross the leaf-choked stream from stone to stone,
  Pass the hoar ash tree, trace the upland path,
The furze-brake that in March all golden shone
  Reflected in the shy kingfisher's bath.

VII.

No more from full-leaved woods that music swells
  Which in the summer filled the satiate ear:
A fostering sweetness still from bosky dells
  Murmurs; but I can hear
A harsher sound when down, at intervals,
The dry leaf rattling falls.
Dark as those spots which herald swift disease
The death-blot marks for death the leaf yet firm:
Beside the leaf down-trodden trails the worm:
  In forest depths the haggard, whitening grass
Repines at youth departed. Half-stripped trees
  Reveal, as one who says, "Thou too must pass,"
Plainlier each day their quaint anatomies.
Yon Poplar grove is troubled! Bright and bold
Babbled his cold leaves in the July breeze
As though above our heads a runnel rolled:
  His mirth is o'er: subdued by old October
  He counts his lessening wealth, and, sadly sober,
Tinkles his minute tablets of wan gold.

VIII.

Be still, ye sighs of the expiring year!
  A sword there is:—ye play but with the sheath!
Whispers there are more piercing, yet more dear
  Than yours, that come to me those boughs beneath;
And well-remembered footsteps known of old
  Tread soft the mildewed mould.
O magic memory of the things that were—
  Of those whose hands our childish locks carest,

Of one so angel-like in tender care,
  Of one in majesty so God-like drest—
O phantom faces painted on the air
  Of friend or sudden guest;—
I plead in vain:
The woods revere, but cannot heal my pain.
Ye sheddings from the Yew tree and the Pine,
  If on your rich and aromatic dust
    I laid my forehead, and my hands put forth
In the last beam that warms the forest floor,
No answer to my yearnings would be mine,
To me no answer through those branches hoar
  Would reach in noontide trance or moony gust!
    Her secret Heaven would keep, and mother Earth
Speak from her deep heart—"Where thou know'st not, trust!"

IX.

That pang is past. Once more my pulses keep
  A tenor calm, that knows nor grief nor joy;
Once more I move as one that died in sleep,
  And treads, a Spirit, the haunts he trod, a boy,
And sees them like-unlike, and sees beyond:
Then earthly life comes back, and I despond.
Ah life, not life! Dim woods of crimsoned beech
  That swathe the hills in sacerdotal stoles,
Burn on, burn on! the year ere long will reach
  That day made holy to Departed Souls,
The day whereon man's heart, itself a priest,
  Descending to that Empire pale wherein

Beauty and Sorrow dwell, but pure from Sin,
Holds with God's Church at once its fast and feast.
Dim woods, they, they alone your vaults should tread,
The sad and saintly Dead!
Your pathos those alone ungrieved could meet
Who fit them for the Beatific Vision:
The things that as they pass us seem to cheat,
To them would be a music-winged fruition,
A cadence sweetest in the soft subsiding:
Transience to them were dear;—for theirs the abiding—
Dear as that Pain which clears from fleshly film
The spirit's eye, matures each spirit-germ,
Frost-bound on earth, but at the appointed term
Mirror of Godhead in the immortal realm.

X.

Lo there the regal exiles!—under shades
Deeper than ours, yet in a finer air—
Climbing, successive, elders, youths, and maids,
The penitential mountain's ebon stair:
The earth-shadow clips that halo round their hair:
And as lone outcasts watch a moon that wanes,
Receding slowly o'er their native plains,
Thus watch they, wistful, something far but fair.
Serene they stand, and wait,
Self-exiled by the ever-open gate:
Awhile self-exiled from the All-pitying Eyes,
Lest mortal stain should blot their Paradise.

Silent they pace, ascending high and higher
The hills of God, a hand on every heart
That willing burns, a vase of cleansing fire
Fed by God's love in souls from God apart.
Each lifted face with thirst of long desire
Is pale; but o'er it grows a mystic sheen,
Because on them God's face, by them unseen,
Is turned, through narrowing darkness hourly nigher.

XI.

Sad thoughts, why roam ye thus in your unrest
The bourne unseen? Why scorn our mortal bound?
Is it not kindly, Earth's maternal breast?
Is it not fair, her head with vine-wreaths crowned?
Farm-yard and barn are heaped with golden store;
High piled the sheaves illume the russet plain;
Hedges and hedge-row trees are yellowed o'er
With waifs and trophies of the laboring wain:
Why murmur, "Change is change, when downward ranging;
Spring's upward change but pointed to the unchanging?"
Yet, O how just your sorrow, if ye knew
The true grief's sanction true!
'Tis not the thought of parting youth that moves us;
'Tis not alone the pang for friends departed:
The Autumnal pain that raises while it proves us
Wells from a holier source and deeper-hearted!
For this a sadness swells above our mirth;
For this a bitter runs beneath the sweetness;

The throne that shakes not is the Spirit's
right;
The heart and hope of Man are infinite;
Heaven is his home, and, exiled here on earth,
Completion most betrays the incompleteness!

XII.

Heaven is his home.—But hark! the breeze increases:
The sunset forests, catching sudden fire,
Flash, swell, and sing, a million-organed choir:
Roofing the West, rich clouds in glittering fleeces
O'er-arch ethereal spaces and divine
Of heaven's clear hyaline.
No dream is this! Beyond that radiance golden
God's Sons I see, His armies bright and strong,
The ensanguined Martyrs here with palms high
holden,
The Virgins there, a lily-lifting throng!
The Splendors nearer draw. In choral blending
The Prophets' and the Apostles' chaunt I hear;
I see the City of the Just descending
With gates of pearl and diamond bastions sheer.
The walls are agate and chalcedony:
On jacinth street and jasper parapet
The unwaning light is light of Deity,
Not beam of lessening moon or suns that set.
That undeciduous forestry of spires
Lets fall no leaf! those lights can never range:
Saintly fruitions and divine desires
Are blended there in rapture without change.

—Man was not made for things that leave us,
  For that which goeth and returneth,
For hopes that lift us yet deceive us,
  For love that wears a smile yet mourneth;
Not for fresh forests from the dead leaves springing,
  The cyclic re-creation which, at best,
Yields us—betrayal still to promise clinging—
  But tremulous shadows of the realm of rest:
    For things immortal Man was made,
  God's Image, latest from His hand,
    Co-heir with Him, Who in Man's flesh arrayed
  Holds o'er the worlds the Heavenly-Human wand:
His portion this—sublime
To stand where access none hath Space or Time,
Above the starry host, the Cherub band,
To stand—to advance—and after all to stand!

Dedicated

TO

THE COUNT DE MONTALEMBERT.

URBS ROMA.

ST. PETER'S BY MOONLIGHT.

Low hung the moon when first I stood in Rome
Midway she seemed attracted from her sphere,
On those twin Fountains shining broad and clear
Whose floods, not mindless of their mountain home,
Rise there in clouds of rainbow mist and foam.
That hour fulfilled the dream of many a year :
Through that thin mist, with joy akin to fear,
The steps I saw, the pillars, last the dome.
A spiritual Empire there embodied stood :
The Roman Church there met me face to face:
Ages, sealed up, of evil and of good
Slept in that circling colonnade's embrace.
Alone I stood, a stranger and alone,
Changed by that stony miracle to stone.

PONTIFIC MASS IN THE SISTINE CHAPEL.

FORTH from their latticed and mysterious cells
The harmonies are spreading, onward rolled:
Ere long, by counter tides met and controlled,
Midway more high the gathering tumult swells.
It sinks—a breeze the incense cloud dispels :—
Once more Sibylline forms, and Prophets stoled
Look down, supreme of Art's high miracles,
Upon the Church terrene. Once more, behold,
With what an awful majesty of mien

The Kingly Priest, his holy precincts rounding,
Tramples the marbles of the sacred scene:—
The altar now he nears, and now the throne;
As though the Law were folded in his zone,
And all the Prophets in his skirts were sounding.

THE PILLAR OF TRAJAN.

Degrading Art's augustest minist'rings,
Yon Pillar soars, with sculptured forms embost,
Whose grace at that ambitious height is lost:
Lo! as the stony serpent twines its rings
Priests, coursers, heralds, warriors, slaves, and kings,
Mingle, a tortuous mass confused and crost;
While Art, least honored here where flattered most,
Deplores in vain her prostituted springs,
By a fallen Angel at their source ill-stirred;
Unholy—thence unhealing!—What is aid,
Vouchsafed, upon conditions that degrade,
To one who her allegiance hath transferred?—
O Attic Art brought low, that here dost stand
Full-fed, but hooded, on a tyrant's hand!

THE ARCH OF TITUS.

I stood beneath the Arch of Titus long;
On Hebrew forms there sculptured long I pored;
Till fancy, by a distant clarion stung,
Woke: and methought there moved that arch toward

A Roman Triumph. Lance and helm and sword
Glittered; white coursers tramped, and trumpets
rung:
Last came, car-borne a captive horde among,
The laurelled Boast of Rome—her destined Lord.
As though by wings of unseen eagles fanned
The Conqueror's cheek, when first that Arch he saw,
Burned with the flush he strove in vain to quell—
Titus! a loftier arch than thine hath spanned
Rome and the world with empery and law;—
Thereof each stone was hewn from Israel!

THE CAMPAGNA SEEN FROM ST. JOHN LATERAN.

WAS it the trampling of triumphant hosts
That levelled thus yon plain, sea-like and hoary;
Armies from Rome sent forth to distant coasts,
And back returning clad with spoils of glory?
Around it loom cape, ridge, and promontory:
Above it sunset shadows fleet like ghosts,
Fast-borne o'er keep and tomb, whose ancient boasts,
By Time confuted, name have none in story.
Fit seat for Rome! for here is ample space,
Which greatness chiefly needs—severed alone
By yonder aqueducts, with queenly grace
That sweep in curves concentric ever on,
(Bridging a world subjected as a chart)
To that great City, head of earth, and heart.

BIRDS IN THE BATHS OF DIOCLETIAN.

EGERIAN warbler! unseen rhapsodist!
Whose carols antedate the Roman spring;
Who, while the old grey walls, thy playmates, ring,
Dost evermore on one deep strain insist;
Flinging thy bell-notes through the sunset mist!
Around thy haunt rich weeds and wall-flowers swing
As in a breeze, the twilight-crimsoning
That sucks from them aërial amethyst—
O for a Sibyl's insight to reveal
That lore thou sing'st of! Shall I guess it? nay!
Enough to hear thy strain—enough to feel
O'er all the extended soul the freshness steal
Of those ambrosial honeydews that weigh
Down with sweet force the azure lids of day.

THE "MISERERE" IN THE SISTINE CHAPEL.

I.

FROM sadness on to sadness, woe to woe,
Searching all depths of grief ineffable,
Those sighs of the Forsaken sink and swell,
And to a piercing shrillness, gathering, grow.
Now one by one, commingling now, they flow:
Now in the dark they die, a piteous knell,
Lorn as the wail of exiled Israel,
Or Hagar weeping o'er her outcast. No—
Never hath loss external forced such sighs!
O ye with secret sins that inly bleed,

And drift from God, search out, if ye are wise,
Your unrepented infelicities :
And pray, whate'er the punishment decreed,
It prove not exile from your Maker's eyes !

THE "MISERERE" IN THE SISTINE CHAPEL.

II.

THOSE sounds expiring on mine ear, mine eye
Was by their visual reflex strangely spelled :
A vision of the Angels who rebelled
Still hung before me, through the yielding sky
Sinking on plumes outstretched imploringly.
Their Tempter's hopes and theirs for ever quelled,
They sank, with hands upon their eyes close-held,
And longed, methought, for death, yet could not die.
Down, ever down, a mournful pageant streaming
Like Souls in whom Despair hath slain Endeavor,
Inwoven choirs to ruin blindly tending,
They sank. I wept as one who weeps while dream-
ing,
To see them, host on host, by doom descending
Down the dim gulfs, for ever and for ever.

A ROMAN LEGEND.—VALERIAN AND CECILIA.

THE eyes that loved me were upon me staying :
The eyes that loved me, and the eyes that won.
Guardian or guide celestial saw I none ;
But the unseen chaplets on her temples weighing

Breathed heaven around! A golden smile was playing
O'er the full lips. Meekly her countenance shone,
And beamed, a lamp of peace, 'mid shadows dun—
Round her lit form the ambrosial locks were swaying.
Fair Spirit! Angel of delight new-born,
And love, unchanging love and infinite,
Aurorean planet of the eternal morn!
That gaze I caught; and, standing in that light,
My soul, from Pagan bonds released by thee,
Upsoared, and hailed its immortality.

ROME AT NOON.

THE streets lie silent, in the shadows deep
Of obelisk and statue o'er them thrown;
A people slumbers in its noonday sleep;
No sound save yon cicala's lazy drone.
Sunshine intense each glittering dome doth steep,
Each Lombard tower, each convent court grass-grown,
Fires the tall arch, and heats each column prone,
My prop in turn as slowly on I creep.
Methinks such stillness reigned that hour in Rome
Three centuries since, when through the fiery air
Uprose, sole-heard, the saintly Pontiff's prayer—
Rose, and a slumbering world escaped its doom.
Vanquished that hour beside Lepanto's shore,
Satan like lightning fell, thenceforth to rise no more.

CHRISTMAS EVE, 1860.

THIS night, O earth, a Saviour germinate:
Drop down, ye heavens, your sweetness from above!
This night is closed the iron book of fate;
Open'd this night the book of endless love.
On from the Orient like a breeze doth move
The joy world-wide—a breeze that wafts a freight
Of vernal song o'er lands benumb'd but late,
Rivers ice-bound, and winter-wasted grove.
Onward from Bethlehem, onward o'er the Ægean,
Travels like night the starry Feast Divine.
All realms rejoice; but loudest swells the pean
From that white Basilic on the Esquiline
Beneath whose roof in sunlike radiance clad
The suffering Father stands—to-night not sad.

THE CATACOMBS.

WHOEVER seeks for penitential days,
And vows that fitly on such days attend,
A region apt, his wanderings here may end:
These caverns, winding in sepulchral maze,
Are stronger than the desert's loneliest ways
Thoughts meek and sad with lofty thoughts to blend:—
Descend, great Pontiff! Sovran Priest, descend!
Let all the Princes of the Church upraise
With annual rites their sceptred hands to God!
Kings of the nations, purpling those strange glooms

With robes imperial, on your faces sink;—
Sink, and be saved, in those dread catacombs!
And deeply of the inspiring incense drink
That rises from the dust the Martyrs trod!

THE APPIAN WAY.

AWE-STRUCK I gazed upon that rock-paved way,
The Appian Road; marmorean witness still
Of Rome's resistless stride and fateful Will,
Which mocked at limits, opening out for aye
Divergent paths to one imperial sway.
The Nations verily their parts fulfil;
And War must plough the fields which Law shall till;
Therefore Rome triumphed till the appointed day.
Then from the Catacombs, like waves, up-burst
The Host of God, and scaled, as in an hour,
O'er all the earth the mountain seats of Power.
Gladly in that baptismal flood immersed
The old Empire died to live. Once more on high
It sits; now clothed with immortality!

ON THE CROSS IN THE INTERIOR OF THE COLISEUM.

FAR from his friends, his country, and his home,
Perhaps on that small spot—ay doubtless there—
Some Christian Martyr fell, in one wide stare
Concentrating the gaze intense of Rome.

Now central stands beneath heaven's mighty dome
The Cross which marks that spot! Stranger, beware!
The Orb of Earth was framed that Cross to bear:
And when, slow-tottering round an Empire's tomb,
These walls, within whose grey encincture vast
That Cross for ages stands as in a shrine,
Around their awful guest shall melt at last,
Each stone descending to the earth, shall say,
"Empires and Nations crumble: but that Sign
Pre-eminent shall stand, and stand for aye!"

THE FOUNTAIN OF EGERIA.

For this cold fount the Sabine Saint and Sage
Wooed by high thought forsook both camp and throne:
Here on his country's weal he mused alone,
Calm-visaged as the planetary page:
That murmuring spring had power his cares to assuage:
Here—dim elsewhere as noontide moon fleece-strewn—
In this religious gloom distinctly shewn,
Egeria shared his kingly hermitage.
O pure as Arethusa, and more high!
Cleaving rough seas she spurned irreverent love;
Thine, Roman Nymph, a tenderer sanctity,
Bending like air that strong white head above
To breathe just counsel in a monarch's ear—
Those kings alone are blest to whom thy voice is dear!

THE MONASTERY OF SAN GREGORIO ON THE CŒLIAN HILL.

As when, descending from that God-led bark
At last on Ararat's broad summit staged,
A ruined earth's sad heir, yet undismayed,
Forth paced, with all his sons, the Patriarch;—
As when above that world of waters stark
He stood, while down they rushed, and standing prayed:—
As when he followed, through some wave-worn glade
With over-arching horns of granite dark,
Advancing without fear he knew not where—
So with his monks went forth from yonder pile
Augustine missioned to that northern isle;
Yon Cœlian Hill descended thus, footbare;
Thus sought a wilderness of hearts all stone;
Thus found a land of death, and made that land his own.

THE GRAVES OF TYRCONNEL AND TYRONE ON SAN PIETRO, IN MONTORIO.

WITHIN Saint Peter's fane, that kindly hearth
Where exiles crowned their earthly loads down cast,
The Scottish Kings repose, their wanderings past,
In death more royal thrice than in their birth.
Near them, within a church of narrower girth
But with dilated memories yet more vast,

Sad Ulster's Princes find their rest at last,
Their home the holiest spot, save one, on earth.
This is that Mount which saw Saint Peter die!
Where stands yon dome stood once that Cross
reversed:
From this dread Hill, a Western Calvary,
The Empire and that Synagogue accurst
Clashed two ensanguined hands—like Cain—in one.
Sleep where the Apostle slept, Tyrconnel and Tyrone!

SONNET.

THE FRANCISCAN CONVENT OF THE ARA CŒLI ON THE CAPITOL.

HERE where of old the Roman Senate sate
Where, thundering from his Capitolian throne,
Co-regent of the Universal State,
Jove o'er that Roman sceptre laid his own,
To-day the sons of Francis, humbly elate,
Keep their aerial nest and vigil lone;
Here, like that bird which "sings at heaven's gate,"
Earliest their Christmas Matin Hymns entone.
Far down, beneath, the Benedictines lie,
Of Orders first;—far down whose Science soared
Highest;*—far down the all-conquering Company†
That raised o'er earth the chalice and the sword:—
But here the meek Franciscans reign on high
That Christ may be in lowliness adored.

* The Dominican Order. † The Company of Jesus.

THE CONVENT OF ST. BUONAVENTURA.

EMBALMED airs, so pure, so fresh, so bland!
Heart-soothing love-note of the dove unseen!
Can such be here? Beyond that leafy screen
Thy ruins, dread Cæsarian Palace, stand!
There, full in face thy cliff-like walls expand,
Man-slaying Coliseum! Tragic scene,
Where, lion-girt, the Martyr stood serene,
And triumphed that strong Faith an Empire banned.
O Rome, thou mystic name for Strength, that hour
Thou knew'st not Strength is none on earth save
Love! *
They knew it, they that, met in yonder bower,
Of Rome spake not, but that fair realm above
Where those who loved and suffered, love and
reign—
Saint Francis, and that warrior Saint of Spain.

SANTA MARIA MAGGIORE.

As stand the Hills around Jerusalem,
As stands the Lord of Hosts around His own,
So stand beside the gates and walls that hem
The Christian Salem with their stony zone
The Seven Basilicas: so stands their gem,
Saint Mary's snowy fane, thy tribute throne,

* "Roma," which signifies Strength, is "Amor," with the letters placed in an inverted order.

O Esquiline, in legends old snow-strewn,
Upreared to her that wears earth's diadem!
Reign, chaste and meek; reign, blissful and benign;
Reign, second Eve, that mortal taint hadst none:
Reign, Maid and Mother of the Child Divine,
For His, not thine, the kingdom thou hast won:
Reign in thy Rome—thy Son's augustest shrine—
And bind her ever closer to that Son!

THE INTERIOR OF ST. PETER'S.

REBELLIOUS Nations! This shall come to pass—
From yonder altar to their kingdoms down
The Kings once more shall pace, sceptre and crown
On that dim sea of marble and of brass,
Showering, as Angels on the sea of glass,
Their amaranthine wreaths! All Powers shall own
A spiritual homage to St. Peter's throne;
Draw thence once more their temporal peace. Alas!
What now are Kings? A thousand years each Nation
Claimed to stand subject to a Father's eye!
All realms invoked the Apostle's arbitration,
An unseen world their strength and unity:—
Proud Kings! proud realms! your victory is your loss!
That rule is brief which rests not on the Cross.

THE MONUMENT OF ST. LEO THE GREAT.

(ATTILA BEFORE ROME.)

LEAGUERING doomed walls—as when on some wild coast
The high-ridged deep, storm-driven from afar,
Makes way in thunder, whitening reef and bar—
Leaguering great Rome, the old world's shame yet boast,
Comes up at last the dread Barbarian host:
To meet them, placid as that ocean star
Whose rising quells the elemental war,
Forth moves, his hands upon his bosom crossed,
That Puissance new, the Church's mitred Sire!
His eye is fixed: as reeds before the breeze
Bending, that host sinks down on suppliant knees:
The standards droop: the trumpet blasts expire:
The "Scourge of God" in heaven his sentence sees;
The embattled Gentiles tremble, and retire.

THE MONUMENTS OF QUEEN CHRISTINA OF SWEDEN AND THE COUNTESS MATILDA.

THIS is the crownless Queen of royal heart;
The Christian Queen that, vowed to Christ, laid down
The infected sceptre and the apostate crown,
Zealous with that dear Lord to bear her part
Whom the blind North was "adverse to desert."

To her what thing was Fortune's smile or frown,
Fortune that stoles the knave, and thrones the clown,
Whose Church the palace is, whose Realm the mart?
Christina, and Matilda! Here they lie!
One spurned a kingdom: dying, one endowed
The meek one with the trappings of the proud,
And fixed her realm, a glittering gem, on high,
Star of that temporal crown by Peter worn—
Sleep well, brave sisters, till the eternal morn!

SIR WALTER SCOTT AT THE TOMB OF THE STUARTS.

I.

THE wild deer, when the shaft is in his side,
Seeks his first lair beneath the forest hoar:
Drawn back from reboant deeps, the exhausted tide
Breathes his last sob on the forsaken shore:
When on the village green the sports have died
The child stands knocking at his Grandsire's door:
So stands by this far tomb of Scotland's pride
Her greatest son, death-doomed, and travel-sore.
So stand, last Singer of the Heroic Age!
Dead are those years so loyal, brave, and high,
That whilome blazoned History's Missal page,
And ring for aye through thy glad minstrelsy:
Old Pilgrim, ended is thy pilgrimag
This hour. The shadows round thee close: now die!

II.

Staff-propt he stands: and all his Country's past
Streams back before his sadly-kindling eye;
King after King, as cloud on cloud, when fast
The storm-rack rushes through the autumnal sky:
Aughrim to Flodden answers! on the blast
Now Mary's, now the Bruce's standards fly:
Those earliest, Irish, kings he sees at last
Cross-crowned on old Iona's shores who lie.
—Thus as he gazed, a voice from vault and shrine
Whispered around him—and from Peter's Tomb—
"Not one alone, but every Royal Line
To my strong Gates, as thou to these, shall come,
Heart-pierced at last; for mine they were; and mine
The Cradles and the Graves of Christendom."

SAINT PETER.

I.

ROCK of the Rock! As He, the Light of Light,
Shews forth His Father's Glory evermore,
So shew'st thou forth the Son's unshaken Might,
Throned in thy unity on every shore.
On thee His Church He built: and though, all night,
Tempests of leaguering demons round it roar,
The Gates of Hell prevail not; and the Right
Shines lordliest through the breaking clouds of war.

Prince of the Apostles! Onward like a wheel
The world rolls blindly, and the nations pant;
But God upon His Church hath set His seal,
Fusing His own eternal adamant
Through all its bastions and its towers in thee—
Luminous it stands through thy solidity.

SAINT PETER.

II.

First of the Faith he made confession sole,
Taught by the Father, not by flesh and blood:
Then He the parts Who strengthens by the whole
Bade him make strong his Brethren, and the rod
Gave him of empire. By that Syrian flood
Lastly, a Love thrice-challenged he confessed
That singly passed the love of all the rest,
And straightway to his hand Incarnate God,
Lifting that Hand which made the worlds, accorded
Rule of His Flock world-wide both fair and pure:
The mystery of His Might in One He hoarded
That all, made one, might live in one secure.
In Christ the Race redeemed is one:—in thee
Forth stands, a Sacrament, that Unity.

www.ingramcontent.com/pod-product-compliance
Lightning Source LLC
LaVergne TN
LVHW020221110826
845151LV00003B/783

* 9 7 8 1 4 2 5 5 3 2 5 1 2 *